THE PURITAN VIEW OF SUBSTANTIVE BIBLICAL LAW

THE PURITAN VIEW OF SUBSTANTIVE BIBLICAL LAW

RELIGION AND LAW SERIES, VOLUME TWO

George J. Gatgounis

WIPF & STOCK · Eugene, Oregon

THE PURITAN VIEW OF SUBSTANTIVE BIBLICAL LAW

Religion and Law Series, Volume Two

Copyright © 2021 George J. Gatgounis. All rights reserved. Except for brief quotations in critical publications or reviews, no part of this book may be reproduced in any manner without prior written permission from the publisher. Write: Permissions, Wipf and Stock Publishers, 199 W. 8th Ave., Suite 3, Eugene, OR 97401.

Wipf & Stock
An Imprint of Wipf and Stock Publishers
199 W. 8th Ave., Suite 3
Eugene, OR 97401

www.wipfandstock.com

PAPERBACK ISBN: 978-1-7252-6119-8
HARDCOVER ISBN: 978-1-7252-6120-4
EBOOK ISBN: 978-1-7252-6121-1

AUGUST 3, 2021

CONTENTS

THE PURITAN VIEW OF SUBSTANTIVE BIBLICAL
LAW | 1

AN OVERVIEW OF PURITAN JURISPRUDENCE | 3
    The Teleology of Puritan Jurisprudence | 4
        The Vision of a National Puritan Utopia | 5
        Sabbath Observance—The Crux of Puritan Social Theory | 6
        The Centrality of Preaching in Puritanism | 9
    Excursus: Congregationalist Puritan Jurisprudence in Practice
        in New England | 11
    Substantive Puritan Law | 11
    The Cohesive Social Order Established by Puritan Law | 15
    A Portait of a Victim of Puritan Jurisprudence:
        Obadiah Holmes | 16
    The Relation of Puritan Covenant Theology and the Puritan
        Sociology | 18
    The Influence of the Puritan War with Charles and the Prelates
        on Puritan Legal Theory | 19
    The Puritan Ideology of Church and State | 22
        Cartwright's Teaching of the Distinction of the Church
            and State | 23
        Cartwright's Teaching on the Relation Between Church
            and State | 26

Cartwright's Teaching on the Nature of Church Government and State Government | 29
Conclusion | 31

JOHN OWEN'S VIEW OF SUBSTANTIVE BIBLICAL LAW | 32

Owen's Description of the Law of God in General | 32
  Owen's Definition of the Law of God | 32
  Owen's View of the Nature of the Law of God | 33
    Owen's Catechism on the Nature of the Law of God | 33
  Owen's View of the Purpose of the Law of God | 34
    Owen's Catechism on the General Purpose of the Law of God | 34
    The Whole of the Law of God Expresses the Holiness of God | 35
    The Whole of the Law of God Expresses the Authority of God | 35
    The Specific Purpose of the Old Testament Law and Sacrifices | 36
  The Function of the Law Negatively Defined | 36
  The Function of the Law Positively Defined | 37
    The Law is "Connatural" to the Sinner | 37
    The Law and Conscience Concur in Their Communication to the Sinner | 38
    The Law Receives Concurrence from the Sinner | 38
    The Law Speaks with Authority | 38
    The Law Contradicts False Notions of Forgiveness | 39
    Owen's View of the Limitations of the Law of God | 39
Owen's Exposition of the Law of God in Particular | 40
  God Is the Sovereign Lawgiver | 40
    The General Distinctions of the Moral Law, Ceremonial Law, and the Law of Christ | 40
    The Laws of Christ Are Executed by His Apostles | 41
  The New Testament Believer's Liberty from the Law | 41
    The New Testament Believer's Liberty from the Ceremonial Law | 41

    The New Testament Believer's Liberty from the Terror of the Moral Law | 42
    The New Testament Believer's Liberty from the Impossibility of Accomplishing Moral Law | 42
    The New Testament Believer's Liberty from the Results of Transgression of the Moral Law | 43
    The New Testament Believer's Liberty from Satan, Sin, the World, and the Claims of Satan, Sin, and the World | 43
The Relation of Christ to the Law of God | 44
The Ceremonial Law of the Old Testament Represented the Glory of Christ | 44
Christ Declared the Spiritual Inward Nature of the Law of God | 44
Christ Is Not a Lawgiver of a New Law | 45 Christ Is the Lawgiver of the Church | 49
The Relation of the Law of God to Creation | 49
    The Created Law of Operation in All of Creation | 49
The Created Law and Light of Nature | 51
    The Law of God Written in the Heart | 51
    Prayer Is a Duty of the Law of Nature | 52
The Relation of the Law of God to Sin | 53
    Indwelling Sin Is a Law | 53
The Knowledge of Sin Is by the Law | 59
    The Function of the Law in General | 59
    Sin Works Violence to the Law of Nature Implanted in Mankind | 59
    Guilt Is the Law Voicing Its Objection to Sin | 60
    The Content of Biblical Law Opposes Sin | 60
    The Law Gives No Strength Against Sin | 65
The Relation of the Law of God to the Gospel | 67
    The Order and Use of Law and Gospel | 67
    The Law's Instrumentality in Conversion | 67
The Relation of the Law of God to Mankind in General | 68
    Why Human Laws Are Often Little Respected | 68
    Laws Designed for the External Establishment of Religion Are Generally Ineffective | 69

The Entire Human Race Is Under the Condemnation of the Law
　　　　of God | 69
　　The Relation of the Law of God to the Regenerate | 71
　　　　The Relation of the Law of God to the Life Calling of the
　　　　　　Regenerate | 71
　　　　The Relation of the Law of God to the Sanctification of the
　　　　　　Regenerate | 71
　　　　The Law Is Given As a Rule of Obedience | 72
　　　　How the Believer Is To Fulfill the Law | 72
　　　　Some Things, Although Lawful, May Become Dangerous If They
　　　　　　Cause Others To Stumble | 73
　　　　Lawfulness of Forms of Prayer | 73
　　Conclusion | 73

THOMAS BOSTON'S VIEW OF SUBSTANTIVE BIBLICAL LAW | 75

　　The Properties of Biblical Law | 75
　　The Purpose of Biblical Law | 76
　　The Penalty for Disobedience to Biblical Law | 77
　　　　Biblical Law and the Covenant of Works | 77
　　　　The Penalty for Breach of the Covenant of Works | 77
　　Three Categories of Biblical Law | 81
　　The Moral Law in Particular | 82
　　　　The Moral Law Before Sinai | 82
　　　　The Relation of the Original Natural Law and the Covenant of
　　　　　　Works | 83
　　　　The Reason the Moral Law Was Given | 87
　　　　Perfect Law-Keeping Necessary To Escape the Wrath of God | 88
　　　　The Law As the Rule of Life for Believers | 89
　　　　The Ten Commandments and Adam's Creation | 90
　　The Difference Between Biblical Law and the Gospel | 91
　　　　Biblical Law Is Partially Inherent; the Gospel Is Not | 91
　　　　The Preaching of the Law Is Necessary, But Only the Gospel
　　　　　　Saves | 91
　　Biblical Law and the Distinction of Church and State | 92
　　Conclusion | 94

Thomas Goodwin's View of Substantive Biblical Law | 94
The Nature of the Law of God | 95
  Definition and Origin | 95
  Purposes | 96
  Components | 97
    Literal and Spiritual Aspects | 97
    Preceptive and Penal Elements | 97
    Moral and Ceremonial Elements | 98
  Characteristics | 99
    Glorious | 99
    Weak on Account of the Flesh | 101
The Function of the Law | 101
  Reflects Divine Honor | 101
  Demands Human Holiness | 103
    Demands Holiness by Universal Testimony | 103
    Demands Holiness by Uniting With and Controlling Conscience | 105
    Demands Holiness by Exposing the Totality of Man's Inner Sinful Nature | 106
    Demands Holiness by Demanding Satisfaction for Violations | 107
    Demands Holiness Through Evangelical Faith and Repentance | 108
    Demands Holiness Through Contemporary Preaching | 111
Christ's Relation to the Law of God | 111
  The Special Law to Which Christ Conforms | 111
  The Perfect Obedience That Christ Rendered | 114
  The Perfect Satisfaction That He Earned | 115
Conclusion | 118

STEPHEN CHARNOCK'S VIEW OF SUBSTANTIVE BIBLICAL LAW | 120
The Relation of the Law of God to God's Nature | 121
  The Relation of the Law of God to God's Incommunicable Attributes | 121
    The Relation of the Law of God to God's Sovereignty | 121

  The Relation of the Law of God to God's Majesty | 122
  The Relation of the Law of God to God's Spirituality | 122
  The Relation of the Law of God to God's Immutability | 123
 The Relation of the Law of God to God's Communicable Attributes | 124
  The Relation of the Law of God to God's Wisdom | 124
  The Relation of the Law of God to God's Mercy | 125
  The Relation of the Law of God to God's Holiness | 126
  The Relation of the Law of God to God's Goodness | 128
 The Relation of the Law of God to Christ the Mediator | 131
 The Relation of the Law of God to the Threefold State of Man—Original, Fallen, and Regenerate | 131
  The Relation of the Law of God to the Original State of Man | 131
  The Relation of the Law of God to the Fallen State of Man | 133
  The Relation of the Law of God to the Regenerate State of Man | 136
 Conclusion | 139

FINAL CONCLUSION | 140

BIBLIOGRAPHY | 143

THE PURITAN VIEW OF SUBSTANTIVE BIBLICAL LAW

Among the many books written on the subject of Puritan history and beliefs, this book finds itself in rare company. Rev. Dr. George Gatgounis, Esq.'s expertise in religion and law is of unquestionable distinction, as is the astonishing depth of research from which this book is derived. While these and many other assets contribute to this study's invaluableness, the most compelling evidence of this work's indescribable worth—positioning it in distinction to others I have read—lies in its usefulness.

The Puritan experiment involved the whole spectrum of personal spirituality interwoven with societal responsibilities. Through Dr. Gatgounis' presentation of the Puritans' common background and the shared gifts, goals, and solutions that spiritually motivated their society, we are able to gain astonishing clarity in understanding the Puritan views that culminated into a vision of harmonious utopia built upon the spiritual well-being of each soul in its community. Furthermore, this work's mature treatment of the righteous motivations of the key luminaries who formed their society explicates the very heart of Puritan sociology.

With amazing intellectual integrity, this work illuminates the Puritan philosophical paths that connect theology with sociology, God's law with man's law, and liberty with obedience, as well as their significant connections to our own contemporary substantive law—and our own convictions.

H. Wayne House

AN OVERVIEW OF PURITAN JURISPRUDENCE

What is the origin of Puritanism? It was an interdenominational movement that continued the Calvinistic Reformation of Christianity throughout the United Kingdom, and later in British Crown colonies. As early as John Jewell and Thomas Cartwright, Calvinistic reformers in the late sixteenth century were seen by their contemporaries as Puritan luminaries. Others of the seventeenth century included Stephen Charnock, Thomas Goodwin, John Owen, Thomas Boston, and Thomas Manton. These Puritans sought an intellectual, moral, and spiritual cleansing of the Church. Their standard of purity was the Bible, that is, the Old and New Testaments solely (Catholicism included the Apocrypha). The Westminster Confession of Faith, written by a symposium of 120 Puritan scholars from 1643-48, expressed Puritan ideas in a comprehensive yet concise manner.

Although this Confession formulated a Presbyterian form of church government, Separatist Puritans, Congregationalist Puritans, and Anglican Puritans alike embraced the theology forwarded by the Confession.[1] Cromwell's Protectorate of 1640-60 ended Puritan hegemony over British political, social, and ecclesiastical institutions. Jonathan Edwards, whose revivalist influence began

---

1. Separatists sought to separate spheres of sovereignty, thus dividing state and church institutions; the Congregationalist, Presbyterian, and Anglican Puritans sought to establish state churches according to their own denominational distinctions.

in earnest in 1739, has been designated the last American Puritan; Puritan hegemony over Massachusetts society, however, ended around 1690, when a remnant of Puritan ideologues transferred from Massachusetts to Connecticut, resulting in the founding of Yale.

THE TELEOLOGY OF PURITAN JURISPRUDENCE

What were the objectives of Puritan jurisprudence? What kind of society did Puritan jurisprudence seek to build? Puritanism sought to produce a society where every individual, family, church, executive, legislature, and court submitted to law as laid down in the Bible. Their hope was for a universal theocracy. Under Puritan ideology, "the spirit of the whole creation was the reformation of the world":

> Reform in all places, all persons and callings. Reform the universities, reform the cities, reform the counties, reform inferior schools of learning, reform the Sabbath, reform the ordinances, the worship of God. Every plant which my heavenly father hath not planted shall be rooted up.[2]

Not only did the Puritans believe that they had received a divine mandate to build a universal theocracy, they believed that such a theocracy was prophesied in the Bible. In other words, they believed that since this kind of society would be established by God anyway; therefore, Puritans should cooperate with God to establish the Kingdom of heaven on earth, and since the same spiritual goals existed for each and every citizen, "progress toward that goal was thought to be a communal affair."[3] Puritan postmillennial

---

2. Sermon to the House of Commons, 1641, quoted in Rosenstock-Huessy, *Out of the Revolution: The Autobiography of Western Man* 291 (1938), in Harold J. Berman, "Religious Foundations of Law in the West: An Historical Perspective," *Journal of Law and Religion*, Volume 1, Number 1, Summer 1983, p. 30.

3. Jude P. Dougherty, "PuritanAspiration, Puritan Legacy: An Historical/Philosophical Inquiry," *Journal of Law and Religion*, Volume 5, Number 1, (1987), p. 113. Compare Thomas Hooker's analogy of the believers' departing

eschatology,[4] therefore, produced a social theory, and thus social theory guided the consequent jurisprudence.

The Vision of a National Puritan Utopia

The Puritan agenda for reform was interconnected, with key elements dedicated to the spiritual reformation of individuals, families, local assemblies, the national church at large, and the commonwealth.[5] An individual, according to Robert Bolton, had not achieved the Puritan vision until that individual walked with God. Bolton defined "walking with God" as a spiritual ideal:

> By walking with God, I mean, a sincere endeavour, punctually and precisely to manage, conduct, and dispose all our affairs, thoughts, words and deeds; all our behaviours, courses, carriage, and whole conversation, in reverence and fear, with humility and singleness of heart, as in the sight of an invisible God, under the perpetual presence of his all-seeing, glorious, pure eye; and by a comfortable consequent, to enjoy by the assistance and exercise of faith, an unutterable sweet communion, and humble familiarity with his holy majesty: In a word, to live in heaven upon earth.[6]

---

from Babylon to journey toward Mount Zion. H.C. Porter, *Puritanism in Tudor England* (Columbia: University of South Carolina Press, 1971), p. 251.

4. The postmillennial system of eschatology holds that the kingdom of heaven will expand on earth until every nation becomes a Christian theocracy. After a period of universal prosperity (material and spiritual) under such a theocratic rule, Christ would return to establish a new heavens and new earth (cf. 2 Peter 3:10; Rev. 20:7–15). The dominant eschatology of the Puritan era was postmillennial, as evidenced by the consensus of Puritan scholars that produced the Westminster Confession of Faith, which included the Larger Catechism. The Larger Catechism's exposition of the Lord's Prayer, particularly the phrase, "thy kingdom come," delineates a postmillennial eschatology.

5. John H. Primus, *Holy Time—Moderate Puritanism and the Sabbath* (Macon, Georgia: Mercer University Press, 1989), p. 168.

6. Robert Bolton, *Some General Directions for a Comfortable Walking with God* (London, 1626), pp. 29–30.

THE PURITAN VIEW OF SUBSTANTIVE BIBLICAL LAW

Not only was the Puritan vision a spiritual metamorphosis of individuals, it included entire families, as Richard Greenham reminds us:

> And surely if men were careful to reform themselves first, and then their own families, they should see God's manifold blessings in our land upon Church and Commonwealth. For of particular persons come families; of families, towns; of towns, provinces; of provinces, whole realms: so that conveying God's holy truth in this sort from one to another, in time, and that shortly, it would so spread to all parts of this kingdom.[7]

The Puritan hope was nothing less than a total metamorphosis of the United Kingdom into a new Israel; furthermore, it was an Israel that would never fall either spiritually or otherwise. To create this society, its citizens were obliged to set aside a day for purposes of preaching and thoughtful reflection.

Sabbath Observance—The Crux of Puritan Social Theory

In order to initiate a spiritual metamorphosis within English society, Puritans wanted to ascend a spiritual ladder that would take the country nearer to God. The foundation of Puritan social theory was strict Sabbatarianism, adherence to the fourth commandment. By a universal observance of the Sabbath for preaching and other spiritual exercises, they intended to amplify the effects of that preaching. John Ley referred to the Sabbath as "the training day of military discipline," observing it was "the sum and substance of all religion."[8] William Gouge held that one's entire personal sanctification depended upon observing it: "The very life of piety is preserved by a due sanctification of the Lord's day. They put a knife to the throat of religion, that hinder the same."[9] Without Sabbath observance, Christians could not fulfill their spiritual

---

7. Richard Greenham, *Works* (1599), p. 164.
8. John Ley, *Sunday a Sabbath* (London, 1641), sig. C4.
9. William Gouge, *The Whole Armour of God* (London, 1627), sig. A2.

potential. "Therefore we might learn to sanctify the Sabbath of the Lord, for else we shall never increase in faith, knowledge, or obedience as we should; for the begetting and increase whereof this day hath been set apart and sanctified from the beginning."[10] A common metaphor for the Sabbath was *marcatura animae*, or "the marketplace of the soul." Henry Burton amplified the metaphor: "Again, it is the market day of our souls, wherein we come to God's house the market place, to buy the wine and milk of the word, without money, or money worth. How is that? By hearing and heeding God's word, that truth whereby we are sanctified, John 17:17, and to pray unto him; thus by the word and prayer we are sanctified."[11] If observing the Sabbath waned, according to George Walker, so would decay all other spiritual exercises: "the most effectual ordinary means of grace and furtherances to eternal life and blessedness, would undoubtedly grow out of use, and at length utterly decay and vanish."[12] To Walker, the Sabbath was "the hedge of defense to true Christian religion." "Preaching, reading and hearing of the word . . . true piety, and the true knowledge and worship of God, and true faith in Christ, are upheld, maintained, increased and continued among all Christian nations from generation to generation."

To Cawdry and Palmer, the Sabbath was a weekly spiritual quintessence, a time when Christians reached their spiritual peak.[13] This zenith represented a victory in the invasion of the kingdom of God on earth. Heaven invaded earth, according to the Puritans' Deuteronomic vision, and without the Sabbath, this would not happen. Henry Burton explains:

---

10. William Perkins, A Godly and Learned Exposition upon Revelation (London, 1606), p. 45.

11. Henry Burton, *The Law and the Gospel Reconciled* (London, 1631), p. 64.

12. George Walker, *The Doctrine of the Sabbath* (Amsterdam, 1638), sig. A2.

13. Daniel Cawdry and Herbert Palmer, *The Christian Sabbath Vindicated* (London, 1645), Epistle to the reader.

so as from the right sanctification of the Lord's day doth spring all holiness, and power of religion, whereby God is honoured, the commonwealth itself is made glorious as being established and combined with the most firm bonds of pure religion, the crown and security of kings and kingdoms.[14]

Cawdry and Palmer saw England's spiritual and material prosperity linked to observing the Sabbath. Failure to do so explained why the English reformation had failed, according to Cawdry and Palmer. "We think one main cause of these national judgments, under which this land now groans, was the public toleration of the profanation of the day."[15] The Puritan historian Primus interprets the "keeping of the Sabbath law" "as the key to all others."[16] Primus continues:

> No wonder that, in their Deuteronomic vision, the welfare of the entire nation would stand or fall with the use or abuse of this holy time, with success or failure in performing the sacred duties of preparing for the Word, hearing the Word, reflecting upon the Word, and "doing" the Word. And no wonder that the appointment of such a critical time could not be left to the relatively untrustworthy discretion of sinful human institutions.[17]

John Sprint captures the expectancy, fervor, and strenuous nature of the phenomenon in his "Ode to the Sabbath."

> A doctrine harmless, true, and holy, making thee holy and preparing thee to heaven, agreeing to the Scripture, to right reason, to common civility, and even to civil policies. A doctrine conforming us to the commandment of God, yea even to his blessed and holy image. A doctrine bringing much glory unto God, and benefit to man, knowledge to the ignorant, sense unto the hardened, direction to the willing, discipline to the

---

14. Burton, Law and Gospel Reconciled, p. 67.
15. Cawdry and Palmer, The Christian Sabbath Vindicated, sig. A2.
16. Primus, p. 180.
17. Ibid.

irregular, conscience to the obstinate, comfort to the conscienced, and bringing none inconvenience in the world. A doctrine that addeth face, fashion, growth and firmitude unto a church, strength and comely order to a commonwealth; giving propagation to the gospel, help and vigor to the laws; ease, honor, and obedience unto the governors; unity and quiet to the people; and lastly, certain happiness and blessing to them all. For the which doctrine whosoever argues, pleadeth for God, for his glory, for his worship, for his commandment and will, for his word, his sacraments, and invocation: for the law, for the gospel, for Moses, and the prophets, for Christ and his apostles, for the upholding and flourishing estate of the church and commonwealth, of schools and universities, and of the faithful ministry of Christ. In a word they plea for the wearied bodies rest, for the evil conscience quiet; for the sound practice of godliness and mercy, in a certain, settled, and constant order. And so by consequence for heaven itself.[18]

Either through responding to a parish sermon or observing law enacted in support of Sabbatarianism, the day was the center of Puritan social reformation.[19]

The Centrality of Preaching in Puritanism

Under Puritanism, "the real energy was supplied by the preacher."[20] "The essential thing in understanding the Puritans is that they were preachers before they were anything else."[21] "In the sermons preached from hundreds of Puritan pulpits . . . Puritan ideology was set forth in its totality."[22] Close personal ties united preachers,

18. John Sprint, *Propositions, Tending to Proove the Necessarie Use of the Christian Sabbaoth, or Lord's Day* (London: Thomas Man, 1607), pp. 35–36.

19. Primus, p. 168.

20. William Haller, *Rise of Puritanism* (New York: Columbia University Press, 1938), p. 15.

21. Irvonwy Morgan, *The Godly Preachers of the Elizabethan Church* (London: Epworth, 1965), p. 11.

22. Paul Seaver, *The Puritan Lectureships* (Stanford: Stanford University

who called each other "brother."[23] The integrity and education of Puritan ministers were a welcomed contrast to other clergy of the period. "Duties neglected, nepotism, plurality, non-residence, self-indulgence, some immorality, and, above all, ignorance—these were characteristic of the Church and clergy."[24]

Only by preaching could clerical abuses and attendant degeneration be halted. No other spiritual exercise equaled the effects of preaching; even a sacrament, such as the Lord's Supper, was a meaningless ritual without the context of preaching.[25] Furthermore, reading the Scriptures without interpretative comment was scorned as a "dumb reading." During the English Reformation, the features of a true church were three: a faithful preaching of the Word, a faithful administration of the sacraments, the Lord's Supper and baptism, and Church discipline. William Whitaker in 1599 went a step further and reduced these to preaching alone.[26]

John More declaimed in Jeremiads a divine judgment against civil rulers if they forbad preachers from parish pulpits. "Unless there be preaching, the people perish: unless they have believed, they are damned, and believe can they not without preaching."[27] Lancelot Andrewes claimed that there could be no political justice without "prophetia,"[28] or "the careful looking to prophecy." Andrewes saw moral declension as the basic cause of the fall of great

---

Press, 1970), p. 5.

23. Actually, the appellation "brethren" connoted Puritanism in their day as much the appellation "comrade" connotes Communism in the present day. Irvonwy Morgan, *Prince Charles's Puritan Chaplain* (Ruskin House: George Allen, 1957), p. 41.

24. Paul A. Welsby, *Lancelot Andrewes* (London: SPCK, 1958), p. 65.

25. John S. Coolidge, *The Pauline Renaissance in England* (London: Clarendon, 1970), p. 142. David Little, *Religion, Order, and Law* (Oxford: Blackwell, 1970), pp. 68–70. John Calvin, *Institutes of the Christian Religion* (Philadelphia: Westminster, 1973), 4:1:5, 4:3:1.

26. William Whitaker, *Praelectiones* (Cambridge, 1599), pp. 387ff.

27. John More, *Three Godly Sermons* (Cambridge, 1594), introduction.

28. The Greek term *prophetia* includes both foretelling and forthtelling. The term encompasses the supernatural apprehension of the future and communication of future events, as well as simple communication of biblical and spiritual concepts.

nations; if a nation attended to the pure preaching of the Word, the nation would retain its political integrity. He illustrated this using a military metaphor. If the enemies of the United Kingdom sought to invade the island, where would they do so? Andrewes believed they would choose the locales "where people are least taught the fear of God."[29]

Andrewes also decried the practice of allowing incompetents to preach:

> Since the dumb-dogs were lately beaten, every dunce took upon him to usurp the pulpit, where talking by the hour glass, and throwing forth headlong their incoherence, they have the luck forsooth to have it called by the name of preaching. The very Church is infested with as many fooleries of discourse as are commonly in the places where they shear sheep.

Of course, the Puritans favored laws that would force society to listen to their preaching; by such persuasion would their ministers saturate society with God's plan.

EXCURSUS: CONGREGATIONALIST PURITAN JURISPRUDENCE IN PRACTICE IN NEW ENGLAND

Substantive Puritan Law

Established by Pilgrims in 1620 and Congregationalist Puritans in 1630, the Massachusetts Bay Colony was essentially a child of England's Congregationalist Puritan sect. The new colony trained its ministers at Cambridge, a center of Puritan thought and practice during this time. In the New World, enacting law was less at the mercy of the enemies created by the Puritan revolution. Unhampered by the factionalism that had occurred in England, the colony was a religious society that was structured around laws derived from the Bible. More than anywhere else, the Puritan concept of the reformation of the world provided a theory of law, and

---

29. Lancelot Andrewes, *The Moral Law Expounded* (London, 1642), pp. 301ff.

it practice, dedicated to religious reformation. The objective was to reform both state and church.

In England, during the 1640s and 1650s, over ten thousand pamphlets were published arguing for legal reforms.[30] The New England Puritans held:

> Whatsoever ordinance of the Old Testament is not repealed in the New Testament, as peculiar to the Jewish Paedagogie, but was of moral and perpetual equity, the same binds us in these days, and is to be accounted the revealed will of God in all ages, though it be not particularly and expressly mentioned in the writings of the New Testament . . . the Scriptures of the New Testament do speak little in these cases; only the Scripture of the Old Testament do give direction and light about them.[31]

The concept of Christian reformation complemented the political doctrine civil law, as we see from this extract (Massachusetts Body of Liberties of 1641):[32]

1. If any man after legal conviction shall have or worship any other God, but the Lord God, he shall be put to death.[33]

2. If any man or woman be a witch, (that is hath or consulteth with a familiar spirit), They shall be put to death.[34]

---

30. Berman, p. 30.

31. *An Apology of the Churches in New England for Church-Covenant* (London, 1643), p. 8, as quoted by John F. Wilson, *Pulpit in Parliament* (Princeton: University Press, 1969), p. 143.

32. Berman, p. 30.

33. Exodus 20:1–6; Deuteronomy 5:6–10. Both previous texts are the narrative record given at Mt. Sinai in Exodus 19. The order of the commandments is significant. The Massachusetts Bay Colony began its basic code of law the same way that the Israelite nation of long ago began theirs—worship of the God of the Bible was the only worship. This canon is in keeping with Exodus 22:20, "he that sacrificeth unto any god, save unto the Lord only, he shall be utterly destroyed."

34. Exodus 22:18: "Thou shalt not suffer a witch to live"; Deuteronomy 18:9–11: "Thou shalt not be found among you anyone who maketh his son or his daughter pass through the fire, or who useth divination, or an observer of times, or an enchanter, or a witch, or a charmer, or a consulter of mediums,

AN OVERVIEW OF PURITAN JURISPRUDENCE

3. If any man shall Blaspheme the name of God, the Father, the Son or Holy Ghost, with direct, express, presumptuous or high handed blasphemy, or shall curse God in the like manner, he shall be put to death.[35]

4. If any person commit any willful murder, which is manslaughter, committed upon premeditated malice, hatred or Cruelty, not in a man's necessary just defense, nor be mere casually against his will, he shall be put to death.[36]

5. If any person slayeth another suddenly in his anger or Cruelty of passion, he shall be put to death.[37]

---

or a wizard, or a necromancer. For all these things are an abomination unto the Lord."

35. Essentially, this third canon in the law of Massachusetts Bay is a particularization of the first. The first canon prohibited worship of any other god; this canon focuses on any evil speaking against the God of the Bible. This canon is an application of Exodus 20:1–6 and Deuteronomy 5:6–10.

Speaking against God was so abominable to the Puritans of Massachusetts Bay that they applied the death penalty. The Puritan application of the death penalty patterns the execution described in Leviticus 24:1–16, 23. Leviticus 24:10–16 records the first implementation of this commandment. In this narrative, "the son of an Israelitish woman" blasphemed the Hebrew God Yahweh. Moses commanded that the party be put in custody until he could inquire of the Yahweh what should be done. Yahweh's verdict was "he who blasphemeth the name of the Lord, he shall surely be put to death" (Leviticus 24:16). In Leviticus 24:23 this judgment was executed against the blasphemer.

36. Genesis 9:6, "Whoso sheddeth man's blood, by man shall his blood be shed." In Exodus 20:13, Moses issues the command prohibiting murder, "Thou shalt not kill." The Hebrew term *hag* may mean any form of killing. However, the term is interpreted in Exodus 21:23, where Moses orders, "Thou shalt give life for life." The Mosaic *lex talionis* required that anyone who took another's life must lose their own. The Exodus 20:13 injunction against murder is repeated in Deuteronomy 5:17.

37. This fifth canon particularizes the fourth. It focuses the colonists' attention upon what we would describe as manslaughter today. The Puritans placed colonists on notice they would not tolerate the violent expression of emotion. Regarding manslaughter, the Puritans applied Exodus 20:13 and 21:23, thus eliminating an entire category of law. To them, capital punishment was an unambiguous response to murder, whatever its origins.

THE PURITAN VIEW OF SUBSTANTIVE BIBLICAL LAW

6. If any person shall slay another through guile, either by poisoning or other such devilish practice, he shall be put to death.[38]

7. If any man or woman shall lie with any beast or brute creature by Carnal Copulation, They shall surely be put to death. And the beast shall be slain and buried and not eaten.[39]

8. If any man lieth with mankind as he lieth with a woman, both of them have committed abomination, they both shall surely be put to death.[40]

9. If any person committeth Adultery with a married or espoused wife, the Adulterer and Adulteress shall surely be put to death.[41]

10. If any man stealeth a man or mankind, he shall surely be put to death.[42]

---

38. This is yet another particularization regarding murder. Whereas in the previous canon, manslaughter was the focus, the sixth turns on two forms of murder: deception and poisoning. Again, the Body of Liberties applied Exodus 20:13 and 21:23.

39. Exodus 22:19 states "Whosoever lieth with a beast shall surely be put to death." The Puritans extended judicial remedies even to animals, indicating hatred of sexual deviation.

40. Deuteronomy 27:20–23 specifies which sexual practices are forbidden. The Puritans applied this, as well as Leviticus 18, proscribing sexual behavior for themselves. These passages forbid marriage with parents-in-law and siblings-in-law. Further, the death penalty applies to homosexuality.

41. Exodus 20:14 is the general moral command against adultery (Deuteronomy 5:18). A New Testament passage, John 8:1–12, poses a seeming contradiction. Yet in John 8, Christ commanded a woman taken in adultery, "Go and sin more." If Christ obeyed biblical law, why would he pardon the woman at the well? One possible resolution of the apparent discrepancy is that Christ acted as a priest in this passage. Priests were to have compassion on those who had fallen out of God's way. Christ functioned as a priest, as distinguished from his role as a king.

42. Exodus 21:16 states that "he that stealeth a man, and selleth him, or if he be found in his hand, he shall surely be put to death."

AN OVERVIEW OF PURITAN JURISPRUDENCE

11. If any man rise up by false witness, wittingly and of purpose to take away any man's life, he shall be put to death.[43]

12. If any man shall conspire and attempt any invasion, insurrection, or public rebellion against our commonwealth, or shall indeavour to surprise any town or Towns, fort or forts therein, or shall treacherously and perfidiously attempt the alteration and subversion of our fame or politics or Government fundamentals he shall be put to death.[44]

This code reflects a Calvinistic schema for determining the relation between church and state, for to the Calvinist, God was king, reigning over both church and state. The magistrate's Address, the General Law of New Plymouth in 1658, states "God being a God of order and not of confusion hath commanded in his word and put man into a capacity in some measure to observe and be guided by good and wholesome laws."[45] Just as the church is regulated by a divine Sovereign, so the state must be regulated also. Puritans called these dictates "liberties," a term that strikes us as ironic today, in these more liberal times. To the Puritans, laws that accorded with the Bible freed them from evil. To the Puritans the terms law and liberty were synonymous.

The Cohesive Social Order Established by Puritan Law

When the Puritans erected their "city upon a hill" in 1629, they established a political texture different from that of other colonies. Conflicting groups from New York and Pennsylvania vied

---

43. The Puritans regarded Exodus 20:13 and 21:23 as inviolable; they applied the death penalty to anyone who would perjure themselves in death penalty cases. If false testimony caused the death of anyone, the party responsible would receive the same sentence.

44. *Colonial Laws of Massachusetts*, compiled by Order of the City Council of Boston, in Charles Dunn, *American Political Theology, Historical Perspective and Theoretical Analysis* (New York: Praeger Publishers, 1984), pp. 22–23.

45. The Address to the General Laws of New Plymouth (1698), 11 Records of the Colony of New Plymouth Laws, 1623–1682, (Pulsifier, ed. 1861), cited by Berman, p. 30.

in the political and economic arena.[46] Meanwhile, the southern royalist colonies endured class violence and a fight for survival; furthermore, their fear of a growing black population alarmed the white aristocracy.[47] In the Bay Colony, however, social unrest was rare; rather, Massachusetts was remarkably cohesive. Differences revolved around religious issues such as the Half-Way Covenant, and policy concerns, such as regulating navigation to appease the Crown.[48] In fact, it was the biblical laws that provided a social amalgam since their severity inspired vigilance. Since the law informed the Massachusetts school system as well, the society developed commonality that bound citizens together.

Unlike Pennsylvania, where the Dutch Reformed taught children in Dutch and Quakers taught according to their creed (Swedish Covenant churches also taught their children according to creed and language), only a small minority of the Massachusetts colonists were not Puritan, and all spoke English. This commonality of creed and language was unique to the Massachusetts colony.[49]

A Portait of a Victim of Puritan Jurisprudence: Obadiah Holmes

It was Obadiah Holmes' misfortune to be a Baptist in a rigidly Puritan Colony, since in 1644 the General Court of the colony had passed a statute against Baptists. The preamble of this resolution includes the following:

> For as much as experience hath plentifully and often proved that, since the first rising of the Anabaptists, about one hundred years since, these have been incendiaries of commonwealths and infectors of persons in the

---

46. William Pencak, *War, Politics, and Revolution in Provincial Massachusetts* (Boston: Northeastern University Press, 1981), p. 2.

47. *Ibid.*

48. William Pencak, *War, Politics, and Revolution in Provincial Massachusetts* (Boston: Northeastern University Press, 1981), pp. 2–6.

49. Thomas Jefferson Wertenbaker, *The Puritan Oligarchy—The Founding of American Civilization* (New York: Charles Scribner's Sons, 1947).

AN OVERVIEW OF PURITAN JURISPRUDENCE

main matter of religion and troublers of churches in all places where they have been.

This indictment of all branches of Anabaptist faith reflected an American Puritan consensus. In conclusion the statute says:

> It is ordered and decreed that if any person or persons within this jurisdiction either openly condemn or oppose the baptizing of infants or shall deny the ordinance of magistracy or their lawful right to punish the outward breaches of the First Table every such person or persons shall be banished from the colony.

In 1649, Obadiah Holmes and other Baptists who worshipped under the Rev. Samuel Newman withdrew and established their own church at Swansea, a town Holmes and his followers named after a small city in Wales.[50] In the year 1651 three Baptists (Clark, the founder and pastor of the Baptist congregation in Newport, Crandall, and Obadiah Holmes) were seized by authorities when the men visited Lynn. The three were accused of propaganda. Crandall and Clark received heavy fines only, but Holmes was imprisoned and later publicly flogged.[51] (A more zealous activist by the name of Endecott advocated the execution of Clark, Crandall, and Holmes.) Holmes complained to Oliver Cromwell, since one of Holmes' associates, a Mr. Leveret, had been a captain of calvary under Cromwell, and Holmes and Leveret thought that Leveret could obtain a favor from Cromwell. The hope vanished when Cromwell responded that "the evil seducers" ought to be banished from the colony.[52]

In general, authorities became increasingly intolerant of divergent opinion. In 1646 Cromwell's Lord's Protectorate passed a law requiring that all heretics "continuing obstinate therein, after due means of conviction, shall be sentenced to banishment." In

---

50. Albert Bushnell Hart, *A Commonwealth History of Massachusetts* (New York: The States History Company, 1927), I:528–29.

51. Hart, I:481.

52. Thomas Hutchinson, *The History of the Colony and Province of Massachusetts Bay* (Cambridge: Harvard University Press, 1936), I:164–65.

1651, when the Cambridge Platform was drafted by the clergy and magistrates, a provision included that "the magistrate is to put forth his coercive power, as the matter shall require" in cases of discipline for heresy.[53] In 1658, the Declaration of Liberties was amended so that no one in the colony who attended a church "which shall be gathered without the approbation of the magistrates and the said churches, shall be admitted to the freedom of this commonwealth.[54] The Puritans therefore, denied freedom to any who did not acknowledge their laws.

THE RELATION OF PURITAN COVENANT THEOLOGY AND THE PURITAN SOCIOLOGY

The Puritan social contract was a religious version of Rousseau's. Rousseau saw this as a meeting of the minds, where those comprising a state decreed the nature of their social order. Rousseau believed the social contract derived from mutual assent between citizens, and that God was not a party to this. To the Puritan, however, God was the initiator and administrator of a binding contract between himself and humankind. The core of the Puritan society was the interconnection between God and all citizens, in order to form a heavenly contract, which consisted of the mutual assent of divine and human participants.[55]

In 1641 the Puritan George Walker wrote that the "word covenant in our English tongue signifies, as we all know, a mutual promise, bargain, and obligation between two parties." Although Walker confines the parties of a covenant to two, his thinking was actually broader. He saw every contract between two individuals as actually a contract between three individuals—the two parties and God.[56] God was part of their daily commerce, as historian Zaret

53. Hart, I:82.

54. Hart, I:481.

55. David Zaret, *The Heavenly Contract—Ideology and Organization in Pre-Revolutionary Puritanism* (Chicago: The University of Chicago Press, 1985), pp. 130–136.

56. George Walker, *The Manifold Wisdom of God* (1641), pp. 39, 40 cited

observes: "... in the form of a heavenly contractor, God became less remote and unknowable. No longer was God unaccountable for God condescended to use a human device, a contract, in his dealings with humanity."[57] Another Puritan, Richard Sibbes, expands on this:

> All the gracious promises of the Gospel are not only promises upon condition, and so a covenant, but likewise the covenant of grace is a testament and a will (a will is made without conditions; a covenant with conditions), that as he has made a covenant what he would have us to do, so his testament is that we shall have the grace to do so.[58]

The concept of a heavenly contract produced a vigilant, active group conscience. Puritans knew that unless they kept the conditions of the heavenly contract, God would repay;[59] if they observed the contract, God would reward. Not only was covenant theology a social ethic that controlled society through laws, but also worked from within, by activating a distinctly Puritan conscience.

THE INFLUENCE OF THE PURITAN WAR WITH CHARLES AND THE PRELATES ON PURITAN LEGAL THEORY

"The first casualty of war is truth," so says the adage, one that those loyal to King Charles leveled at Puritan lawyers and ministers who by their sermons to Parliament became its legal ideologues and social policymakers. The Puritan revolution entailed a violent clash of worldviews. What began as an effort to free the pulpits from the Papacy and other manifestations of Rome developed into war to destroy the prelacy and monarchy. The status quo was represented

---

by Zaret, p. 169.

57. Zaret, pp. 167–68.

58. Richard Sibbes, Christ's Exaltation Purchast by Humiliation, in *The Works of Richard Sibbes* (1639), 5, 342, as quoted by Zaret, p. 169.

59. Zaret, p. 169.

by the monarchy and the prelacy. When King James I was confronted with Millenary Petition in 1608, where 1,000 Presbyterian Puritans signed a petition for an English Presbyterian church, the King shouted "I will harry them out of the land." To James, who was supreme head of the Anglican state church (thanks to Elizabeth's Act of Supremacy), "no bishop" meant "no king." On the other side, the Puritans, by whatever means necessary, sought to replace a corrupted system of authority with a new authority structure built around a Calvinistic model of the church-state. Each side claimed to be "champions of law."[60] Each side accused the other of "setting themselves above law and usurping the sovereignty of the state."[61] Although King Charles I blamed the disaffection of his subjects upon Puritan preachers, Puritan lawyers came to evoke public opinion just as vigorously, particularly at commencement of hostilities in March 1642.[62] The break between Charles and Parliament resulted in a plethora of Puritan declarations, manifestos, and pamphlets on law and religion,[63] including a pamphlet that called into question the presumptions of divine right:

> A question answered: How Laws[64] are to be understood, and obedience yielded. The answer was that there is in Laws an equitable, and literal sense. Command of the militia may be entrusted by law to the king for the public good to serve which is the reason and equity of law. But when any commander whatever acts contrary to the public good, then he himself gives liberty to the Commanded to refuse *obedience* to the Letter. Not need this *equity* be expressed in the Law, being so naturally implied and supposed in all Laws. Parliament cannot be required to vote its own destruction. A general may not turn his guns on his own men. Were he to do so, he

60. William Haller, *Liberty and Reformation in the Puritan Revolution* (New York: Columbia University Press, 1955), p. 72.

61. Haller, p. 72.

62. Haller, pp. 71, 73.

63. Haller, p. 73.

64. Capitalization, italics, and spelling are true to the original in this quotation.

AN OVERVIEW OF PURITAN JURISPRUDENCE

would *ipso facto* estate them in a right of disobedience, except we think that obedience binds Men to cut their own throats.[65]

The reference to suicide is seminal to Puritan thinking. If the King, who ruled by divine right, ordered a subordinate to cut his own throat, even the ignorant would conclude that the command cannot emanate from God because suicide, as self-murder, violates the sixth commandment. The Puritan worldview presupposes a higher law than man's; through understanding the Bible and their own consciences, subjects are acquainted with higher law. To Puritans, law was all-powerful. They believed that as God gave the law to Moses to govern Israel, and God gave nations his law in the Bible as well, this law took precedence over kings and subjects alike. Not only had Christians the right, but the responsibility, to obey God's law rather than man's, if they contradicted each other.[66] If a monarch ruled, this was the tyranny of monarchy; if a group ruled, this was the tyranny of oligarchy; if the majority ruled, this was tyranny of the majority. When God ruled, however, to the Puritan mind this was liberty.

Prior to the revolution, the doctrine of higher law had found a powerful exposition in Christopher St. German's *Dialogue in English, betweene a Doctor of Divinitie, and a Student in the Lawes of England,* (commonly referred to as *The Doctor and the Student*). St. Germain's work held the greatest sway upon the lawyers and lawmakers of the Puritan era. The overarching idea that

65. *A Question Answered*, dated April 21, 1642, as quoted by Haller, p. 73.

66. In this respect the Puritans surpassed their theological mentor, John Calvin. Calvin held that it was the right of Christians to rebel against a religiously oppressive government but not their responsibility. Calvin's view of the right of Christians to rebel is qualified, however; only the Christian magistrate, as a representative of Christian subjects, had the right to resist tyranny. "To withstand the fierce licentiousness of kings," Calvin wrote, lower magistrates, as protectors of the community under them, are to have the divine right and duty of constitutional resistance to tyranny. John Knox, Calvin's pupil, was one of the second-generation reformers who moved a step beyond Calvin. Knox believed it was not only the option but the duty of Christians to rebel against a government that did not submit to the higher law. John Calvin, *Institutes of the Christian Religion* (Phil.: Westminster Press, 1973), IV:20, pp. 1518–19.

circumscribed his works was that courts of equity, by setting up rules of equity based upon the Bible, universal reason, and conscience, could "supply inadequacies and correct injustices arising under the laws of states."[67] St. German taught English lawyers that God "imprinted the law of nature in every man, teaching him what is it be done, and what is to be fled. This law must be obeyed upon peril of one's soul, and it cannot be contravened by human custom, enactment, or decree."[68] Accordingly, the English common lawyer John Lilburne, a member of Parliament throughout the 1640s, would enter the House of Commons with his Bible in one hand and the *Institutes* in the other.[69] Parliament seized upon this doctrine in order to justify its crusade against Charles I. Parliament, and those who supported it, saw this governing body as the embodiment of divinely given law, supervening the corrupted rule of monarchy.

THE PURITAN IDEOLOGY OF CHURCH AND STATE

In Cambridge of the late sixteenth century, a Puritan luminary emerged who pioneered the distinctives of the Presbyterian branch of English Puritanism, which represented a consensus regarding the roles of church and state. Cartwright's view of these is derived from Calvin's *Institutes*, the most widely read theology of both the sixteenth and seventeenth centuries.[70] From Thomas Cartwright

   67. Haller, p. 72.
   68. Haller, p. 72.
   69. Berman, p. 33.
   70. "No other theological work was so widely read and so influential from the Reformation to the American Revolution. At least seventy-four editions in nine languages, besides fourteen abridgments, appeared before the Puritan exodus to America, an average edition annually for three generations." In 1578, the *Institutes* and Calvin's Catechism were required of all Oxford undergraduates. Until Archbishop Laud's supremacy in the 1630s, the *Institutes* was the key theological treatise in England among Anglicans and the various Puritan sects. Even Laud spoke subdued praise for the *Institutes*: the *Institutes* "may profitably be read as one of their first books of divinity." But Laud cautioned

is derived the Puritan distinction separating church and state, as well as the relationship connecting church and state, and nature of church government and state government.

Cartwright's Teaching of the Distinction of the Church and State

The historical origins of the English Puritan movement were predicated on the eclipse of the church. Beginning with Henry the Eighth's reign, the monarch of England was also the head of the English state church, according to the Act of Supremacy; hence all political, legal, and ecclesiastical activities were under the auspices of the Crown. This eclipse of church sovereignty by the state prompted one late 16th-century theologian, Whitgift, to state:

> If the church and commonwealth were under a Christian Prince all one:[71] it should follow, that whosoever is a part of one, should needs be a part of the other: and contrawise, whosoever is cut of from one, must be cut of from the other.[72]

Whitgift's view of church and state as one inspired Thomas Cartwright of Cambridge to respond according to the Calvinist "two kingdoms" doctrine.[73] Although Cartwright views both

---

against New College students from reading it "so soon." "I am afraid it... doth too much possess their judgment... and makes many of them humorous in, if not against the church." Herbert D. Foster, *Collected Papers* 78 (privately printed, 1929), as quoted by Berman, p. 25.

71. Spelling in this quotation is true to the 16th-century original.

72. A. F. Scott Pearson, *Church and State—Political Aspects of Sixteenth Century Puritanism* (Cambridge: At the University Press, 1927), p. 10. Note that Cartwright's works have been out of print since the 19th century; therefore, all quotes issue from Pearson's work, *Church and State*.

73. The Roman Catholic doctrine of the "two swords" evolved, under the Calvinistic phase of the Protestant reformation, into the "two kingdoms." The phrase "two swords" first appeared in a letter from Pope Gelasius I to Emperor Anastasius in the late 400s, where the Pope held that the imperial sphere of social order and lawmaking belonged to the Emperor and the spiritual sphere of spirituality belonged to the Pope. Boniface VIII, however, in 1302 ascribed

church and state as thoroughly religious entities, he did not view them as one. Cartwright proposes that the "church and state should be two self-sufficient complete and distinct, but related societies."[74] Cartwright defends his thesis by texts from the Old Testament, using the words of Christ, the Apostolic Church, and post-Apostolic church fathers. According to Cartwright's interpretation, the Judaean King Jehoshaphat set a normative example of church-state relations in 2 Chronicles 19:11, appointing separate functionaries over ecclesiastical and governmental duties. Some officials were given authority over "all matters of the Lord," others over "all the king's matters."[75] According to Cartwright, 2 Chronicles 19:11 forbad an individual from holding an ecclesiastical and political office simultaneously. Earlier, John Jewel argued that an individual could hold ecclesiastical and political office simultaneously. Jewell points out that Samuel, although a prophet *to* Israel, was also a judge *over* Israel. To this example (including other Old Testament prophets who were rulers also, including Abraham, David, and Solomon), Cartwright responds:

> Some sharper Adversary[76] might here have objected: that Moses, David, and Solomon, being princes in the most flourishing estate of the church: did notwithstanding make church orders. Whereunto I answer, that they did so, partly, for that they were not kings only and princes, but also prophets of God: partly, for that they had special and express direction thereto from god by the prophets: whereby they did even those things in the church, which,

---

both spheres to be ruled by the Pope, who wielded both secular or temporal and ecclesiastical or spiritual swords. Bearman, p. 15. Calvin taught the theory of the two kingdoms, but the church and state were each severally responsible to God. After Cartwright, the Scottish Presbyterian Puritan Samuel Rutherford wrote *Lex Rex*, where he appealed to the law of nature written upon the hearts of all mankind, the ultimate sovereignty of the people, the origin of government in a covenant between God, the governor, and the governed, and the right of resistance when that covenant was broken. Later, John Locke would coin the Calvinistic political arguments in the late 1680s and 1690s.

74. Pearson, p. 10.

75. Pearson, p. 11.

76. Spelling, punctuation, and capitalization are true to the original.

AN OVERVIEW OF PURITAN JURISPRUDENCE

without such special revelation, was not lawful for the priests themselves to have done. And although the truth of this answer be apparent: yet, that it may have the more authority, especially with the D[octor] that tasteth nothing without this sauce; he may understand that it is M. Calvin's answer of Moses, and that in this present cause now debated.[77]

Cartwright's view of overlapping ecclesiastical and political powers (Moses, David, and Solomon, for example) makes a distinction between "extraordinary" and "ordinary" offices in Scripture. The former were filled by those endowed with a supernatural ability, with knowledge of the future and the power to perform miracles. On the other hand, ordinary officers included those who, like the Levitical priests, fulfilled their duties ordinarily, that is, devoid of any supernatural knowledge or ability. Citing quotations from Christ, Cartwright argues that church and state were distinct entities. Christ's example, according to Cartwright, defines the distinction: "our Savior Christ, having the spirit without measure, refused as a thing unmete for his minstery, the office of a Judge."[78] In defense, Cartwright quotes Luke 12:13–14, "Master, bid my brother divide the inheritance with me." Christ responds, "Man, who made me a judge or a divider over you?" Cartwright deduces from this that ecclesiastical officials should not meddle in matters of civil authority.[79] Using Matthew 20:25, Mark 10:42, and Luke 22:25, Cartwright cites Christ's admonition to the sons of Zebedee's wife that they should not exercise dominion as the princes of Gentiles do, but seek to be the servant of all.[80] When Christ refuses to administer a civil judgment in the case of a woman taken in adultery (John 8:1–12), Cartwright deduces that the refusal was tantamount to a separation of ecclesiastical from judicial authority. Moses would have put the woman to death because he was supreme judge of the fledgling state of Israel in 1446 b.c.;

---

77. Pearson, p. 12.
78. Pearson, p. 10.
79. Pearson, p. 10.
80. Pearson, p. 11.

Christ forgave the woman because he was head of a spiritual and ecclesiastical entity, the Christian church of a.d. 30. Cartwright also argues, using the Apostles as his example, that church and state are distinct entities in the biblical sense. He draws a dubious analogy on this point, however. Since elders are endowed with spiritual gifts, but earthly matters were relegated to deacons, so ecclesiastical matters belonged to the church and civil matters to the state. In speaking against "mingling of civil and ecclesiastical estates," Cartwright mentions the post-apostolic father Ambrose, who would not allow doctrinal issues to be deliberated in civil courts. Cartwright further identifies his position as opposite to that of Augustine, differing also with his own contemporaries, the reformers Calvin, Beza, and Bucer.[81] In sum, Cartwright argues that a minister should not concurrently serve as a judge, because the ministerial function

> is of greater weight than the strongest back can bear, of wider compass then the largest handes can faddam: a soldiarfare that will be only attended upon: seeing also it tendeth to the destruction of the body when one member encroacheth upon the office of another: and the civil Magistrate may by the same right invade the office of the Minister as he the office of the civil Magistrate.[82]

Cartwright's Teaching on the Relation Between Church and State

Cartwright's analysis of the relationship between church and state argues the church's superiority. The state is healthy only while the church is healthy: "the church is the foundation of the world, and therefore the common wealth builded upon it."[83] In 1647, another Puritan, Samuel Richardson, framed the issue of which should dominate the other: "either the civil, or the spiritual state must

---

81. Pearson, pp. 13–14.
82. Pearson, p. 14.
83. Pearson, p. 17.

be supreme: which of these must judge the other in spiritual matters?" To Richardson, the ecclesiastical realm takes precedence over the political.[84] Similarly, Cartwright sees the primacy of the church over society:

> As the house is before the hangings and therefore the hangings which come after must be framed to the house which was before, so the church being before there was any commonwealth, and the commonwealth coming after must be fashioned and made suitable unto the church. Otherwise God is made to give place to men, heaven to earth.[85]

Cartwright calls on magistrates to "submit their scepters, to throw down their crowns before the church,"[86] believing that the state exists to provide an orderly and efficient environment for the church to fulfill her mandate by gathering the "full number of the elect."[87] Cartwright analogizes the relation of church and state through allusion to the mythological twins of Hippocrates. When one twin laughs, the other laughs; when one weeps, the other weeps,[88] meaning that when the church is negligent, her negligence results in some cognizable wound in the state, or as Pearson states his summary of Cartwright's view: "deficiencies of the one produce deficiencies in the other. The commonwealth will not flourish until the church is reformed."[89] Cartwright's analogy

---

84. Samuel Richardson, *The Necessity of Toleration in Matters of Religion*. King's Pamphlets, E. 407 (18), p. 11, as quoted by G.B. Tatham, *The Puritans in Power upon it—A Study in the History of the English Church from 1640 to 1660* (Cambridge: At the University Press, 1913), p. 215.

85. Pearson, pp. 16–17. For too long Puritan ministers were limited by the civil laws of Anglican-controlled offices. For examples of how Puritan ministers circumvented these restrictions, see Ronald D. Marchant, *The Puritans and the Church Courts in the Diocese of York, 1560-1642* (Aberdeen: Longmans, 1960), pp. 83ff.

86. Margo Todd, *Christian Humanism and the Puritan Social Order* (Cambridge: Cambridge University Press, 1987), p. 195.

87. Pearson, p. 17.

88. Pearson, p. 19.

89. Pearson, p. 20.

of the Hippocrates twins implies that church and state are symbiotically bound together. The church depends upon the state to provide an external social order, under which the church spreads the Gospel and even disciples its adherents. Cartwright compares the need of the state for the church to the need of all life for the sun.[90] The state needs the church, whose duty it is to change citizens from within, into governable, law-abiding, and contributing members of society. A commonwealth "without the church cannot long survive," Cartwright declaimed.[91] If the church's message (God's word) is "despised or abridged of a free and full course, princes, magistrates, and their commonwealths go to wreck or decay." "The want of the word of God produces a corresponding want of prosperity in the state."[92] Defending this view, Cartwright cites Proverbs 8:15 and Isaiah 60:12 "by me[93] kings reign, and princes decree justice"; "for nation and kingdom that will not serve thee shall perish." Cartwright (as quoted by Whitgift) furthers his argument by drawing on Proverbs 8:15 and Isaiah 60:12:

> It is true that we ought to be obedient unto the civil magistrate which governeth the church of God in that office which is committed unto him and according to that calling. But it must be remembered that civil magistrates must govern it according to the rules of God prescribed in his word, and that as they are nurses so they be servants unto the church, and as they rule in the church so they must remember to subject themselves unto the church, to submit their sceptres, to throw down their crowns, before the church, yea, as the prophet spaketh [Isaiah 49:23],[94] to lick the dust of the feet of the church.

90. *Ibid.*, p. 20.

91. Ibid.

92. Pearson, pp. 20–21.

93. Most Christian commentators of Proverbs 8 hold that the discourse's subject is Christ. This text would be interpreted "by Christ kings reign." In Cartwright's worldview, Christ cannot be known except through his disciples who communicate the Word.

94. Isaiah 49:23: "And kings will be your guardians, and their princesses your nurses. They will bow down to you with their faces to the earth, and lick the dust of your feet; and you will know that I am the Lord; those who

Wherein I mean not that the church doth either wring the sceptre out of the princes' hands, to take their crowns from their heads, or that it requireth princes to lick the dust of her feet (as the pope under this pretense hath done), but I mean, as the prophet meaneth, that whatsoever magnificence, or excellency, or pomp, is either in them, or in their estates and commonwealths, which doth not agree with the simplicity and (in the judgment of the world) poor and contemptible estate of the church, that they will be content to lay down.[95]

Cartwright's conception of any government official, whether a hereditary monarch or elected, is that the official is chiefly a servant of God. Earthly rulers must obey the commands of God in the Scriptures.[96] (Were Cartwright alive today, some would call him a theonomist or Christian reconstructionist.)[97]

Cartwright's Teaching on the Nature of Church Government and State Government

Cartwright's most significant contribution to the Puritan movement is his exposition and apologetics for Presbyterian government, developed in lectures at Cambridge on the Book of Acts. His method is *ad fontes*, "return to the sources," that is, the books of the Bible.[98] His influence on Presbyterianism earned him recognition as the father of Presbyterian Puritanism. Cartwright believes that both the church and state were theocracies.[99] The government

hopefully wait for me will not be put to shame."

95. Pearson, p. 26 quoting the *Works of John Whitgift*, volume 3, p. 189.

96. Pearson, pp. 26–27.

97. For an overview of the theonomic or Christian reconstructionist framework, see Greg Bahnsen, *Theonomy in Christian Ethics* (Philipsburg: Craig Press, 1979).

98. William Furke, *Elizabethan Puritanism* (New York: Oxford University Press, 1971), p. 235.

99. He believed, however, that the Presbyterian church should be the church of the entire nation. C. E. Whiting, *Studies in English Puritanism from the Restoration to the Revolution* (New York: Augustus M. Kelley Publishers,

of the state and the government of the church are coterminous under one governor, who is God. The framework of the ecclesiastical government that Cartwright fashions from the Book of Acts was fundamentally anti-monarchy, his framework democratic and republican. It was democratic in that he believed that congregations should have a say in the determination of their ministers. Writing on the election of an assembly's ministers, Cartwright argued:

> Which things, if they have grounds in civil affairs, they have much better in ecclesiastical. For it is much more unreasonable that there should be thrust upon me a governor of whom the everlasting salvation or damnation both of my body and soul doth depend, than him of whom my wealth and commodity of this life doth hand; unless those upon whom he were thrust were fools, or madmen, or children, without all discretion of ordering themselves.[100]

It was up to congregations to vote for ministers who would represent them. Further, these elected ministers should meet in higher bodies called presbyteries to vote on matters of church dogma and praxis. Similarly, Cartwright asserts that political sovereignty should depend on the consent of the governed:

> It is said among lawyers and indeed reason, which is the law of all nations, confirmeth it, *Quod omnium interest ab omnibus approbari debet:* 'That which standeth all men upon should be approved of all men. Which law hath this sense, that if it may be, it were good that those things which shall bind all men, and which require the obedience of all, should be concluded, as far as may be, by the consent of all, or at least by the consent of as many as may be gotten. And therefore it draweth much the obedience of the subjects of this realm, that the statutes, whereby the realm is governed, pass by the consent of the most part of it, whilst they be made by them whom the

1968), p. 46.

100. Pearson, p. 45 quoting the *Works of John Whitgift*, volume 1, 372.

rest put in trust, and choose for that purpose, being as it were all their acts.[101]

Clearly, the consent of the governed, both in ecclesiastical and political spheres, was a hallmark of Cartwright's theory of legal and political sovereignty.[102] Jeremiah Burroughes, an influential commentator on the Book of Ezekiel, supported Cartwright's viewpoint when he wrote that no Christian was bound to obey a government "that he no way ... hath ... yielded consent unto."[103]

CONCLUSION

Modern adherents of Calvinistic theology may mourn the passing of the Puritan era. But, as Harold J. Berman of Harvard remarks, a future focus is in order:

> Merely to mourn the passing of an era would, of course, be foolish. Since there is no going back, the important question is, "How shall we go forward?" By retracing the experience through which we arrived at our present predicament, can we find some guidelines, and some resources, that may help us to overcome the obstacles that block our way to the future?[104]

101. Pearson, p. 44, quoting the *Works of John Whifgift*, volume 1, 370.

102. There were clear limitations to the application of this principle. Cromwell, for instance, demonstrated no concern regarding the consent of Catholic Ireland when he instituted rule by the sword. The northern province, Ulster, openly embraced Puritanism while the southern provinces remained Papist. Cromwell held the Papists to be heretics and idolaters unworthy of any role in self-government. Further, Cromwell's subjugation of the Irish Papists was so severe that for decades the most fearful imprecation the Irish could hurl at each other was "the curse of Cromwell be upon you." John Stephen Flynn, *The Influence of Puritanism on the Political and Religious Thought of the English* (New York: E.P. Dutton, 1920), p. 93.

103. Jeremiah Burroughes, as quoted by Paul S. Seaver, *Journal of Church and State*, Volume 26, Number 1, Winter 1984, p. 136. Seaver quotes Donald and Keith Thomas, ed., *Puritans and Revolutionaries: Essays in Seventeenth-Century History Presented to Christopher Hill* (Oxford: Clarendon Press, Oxford University Press, 1982).

104. Berman, p. 42.

JOHN OWEN'S VIEW OF SUBSTANTIVE BIBLICAL LAW

Some historians refer to John Owen as "prince of Puritan divines," since his influence exceeded other Congregationalist luminaries. His scholarship is involved with a tone of certainty, derived in part from the scope of his learning, as well as from his reverence for the Word of God, and his desire to see all Scripture interrelated. Owen's treatment includes an exposition of the text itself, and in addition a system of related texts. His spiritual incisiveness and insight make him a Christian scholar of value and reputation.

OWEN'S DESCRIPTION OF THE LAW OF GOD IN GENERAL

Owen's Definition of the Law of God

Owen's definition of the law of God is simple yet profound. "The law is the beam of the holiness of God himself." Whatever the law of God communicates to anyone, it does so in the name and authority of God. Biblical law, therefore, is both "of God" and "from God." Biblical law is "of God" because its content is a direct reflection of who and what God is. Biblical law is the character of God recorded in writing, but also it comes "from God."[1] The source of

---

1. John Owen, ed. William Gould, *The Works of John Owen* (London: Johnstone and Hunter, 1851), VI:389.

biblical law is not the people, and neither is it from any particular religious organization. Rather, the source of biblical law is unique because it issues from God alone.

Owen's View of the Nature of the Law of God

Owen's Catechism, a profound complement to the Westminster Divines' Smaller Catechism, though not equal in length to the Larger Catechism, covers both the nature and the purpose of the law of God.[2] Owen explicates his views of the nature of God's law by answering a series of related questions.

Owen's Catechism on the Nature of the Law of God

In his catechism, Owen's first question on the law of God is "Which is the law that God gave man at first to fulfill?" He answers that the law of God did not begin at Mount Horeb in Exodus 20 but rather with the creation of Adam, adding that the reason this law has binding authority has nothing to do with it being given to the Israelites. Rather, Owen argues that the law of God binds all mankind because it is written on our hearts by the finger of God as part of his creative work. He argues this from the *locus classicus* Romans 2:14, 15.[3]

Owen's second question follows from the first. There are five passages that he appropriates to show the "uttermost tittle" of the law of God is still required of us: Matthew 5:17, 1 John 3:4, Romans 3:31, James 2:8–10, and Galatians 3. (1) Matthew 5:17 establishes the abiding validity of the law. Owen chooses this passage because it is the thesis of Christ's first sermon (Matthew 5–7). Christ did not come to destroy the law but to "fill it to the full (πληρῶσαι)."[4] (2) Owen's choice of 1 John 3:4 is a skillful use of arguing from the obverse. The text contends that sin is the transgression of the law.

---

2. I:476.
3. I:476.
4. I:476.

Since sin is forbidden in every detail, then the obverse of sin, which is conformity to the law, must also be comprehensive.[5] (3) In Romans 3:31, Paul clearly states that Apostolic teaching does not void the law; rather, Apostolic teaching establishes it.[6] (4) James 2:8–10 further elucidates the authority of the law, for to violate the least point of the law is to break it entirely.[7] (5) Galatians 3 discusses the relationship between God's law and the doctrine of justification by faith, in particular (Galatians 3:21), stating that the doctrine does not contradict the Gospel, and vice versa.[8]

Owen's third question involves the power that is required to keep the law. He argues from the perspective of distinct natures that fallen man cannot keep the law. Law is spiritual, whereas fallen man is carnal.[9]

In his fourth question Owen defends God's propriety as lawmaker. Although fallen man cannot keep the law, he once had the capacity to keep the law when God first gave it. Adam and Eve were created with the law of God written upon their hearts, according to Owen, who draws on Genesis 1:26, Ephesians 4:19, Romans 5:12 to establish that man once had the capacity to keep God's law.[10]

Owen's View of the Purpose of the Law of God

Owen's Catechism on the General Purpose of the Law of God

Owen's fifth and sixth catechism questions pertain to the purpose of God's law. By this question, he concludes that the law has two objectives of a general nature (Psalm 19:7–11; 1 Timothy 1:8–9;

---

5. I:476.
6. I:476.
7. I:476.
8. I:476.
9. I:476. In support Owen cites 1 Kings 8:46; Gen. 6:5; John 15:5; Rom. 7:14; 8:7; 1 John 1:8.
10. I:476.

Galatians 3:24). First, we must discover what obedience to God entails. Second, observing the law drives us to Christ.[11]

In his sixth question, Owen explains how God's law inclines us to Christ. Owen sees the law of God beckoning us to Christ in three ways: (1) by "laying open . . . the utter disability of our nature to do any good (Romans 7:7–9 and Galatians 5:19–21), (2) by charging the conscience with the "wrath and curse of God, due to sin" (Romans 3:19–20; 4:15; 5:20); (3) by bringing the soul into bondage to sin, to Satan, death, and hell. This bondage makes us "long and seek for a Savior."[12]

The Whole of the Law of God Expresses the Holiness of God

Just as the law expresses the authority of God, so it speaks to his holiness. Being exposed to the holiness of God results in shame for the sinner, comprised of a sense of the filth of sin. Owen calls this "poena damni,"[13] referring to any lack of conformity to the law of God as "macula" (spot, stain, and filth), because the law expresses God's holiness.[14] Owen sees both the fear and shame produced by the law as "perverse disorder and shameful crookedness," allowing one to compare law's purity with the filth of sin.[15]

The Whole of the Law of God Expresses the Authority of God

Because the law expresses the authority of God, as Owen explains, "guilt inseparably follows every sin."[16] Even though the act of sinning may diminish in time, the guilt of the act remains, a residual, continuing guilt that produces fear. Fear is an expression of guilt, says Owen. He notes that Adam spoke of fear because he was guilty.

11. I:476.
12. I:476. Owen cites in support Galatians 3:22; Hebrews 2:15.
13. III:428.
14. III:428.
15. III:428.
16. III:428.

"I heard thy voice, and I was afraid" (Genesis 3:10). The authority of God, as embedded in the law, produces fear in the sinner, which Owen call "peona sensus."

The Specific Purpose of the Old Testament Law and Sacrifices

Owen sees that Old Covenant sacrifice is designed to remedy the guilt of sinners. "In the doctrine of the law, with the sanction and curse of it, and the institution of sacrifices to make atonement for sin, God declared the nature of guilt and its remedy."[17] The Old Covenant law and sacrifices provide object lessons regarding the nature of guilt, and how God may remove that guilt.

The Function of the Law Negatively Defined

According to Owen, the law cannot demonstrate forgiveness nor dispense mercy. The sanctions of the law, in their entirety, lie against the sinner, speaking with simplicity and finality, such that there is no mercy. To support this proposition, Owen cites both Deuteronomy 27:26 and Galatians 3:10, "cursed is he that continueth not in all things in the book of the law to do them." Further, as Paul explains in Galatians 3:10, those who "are under the law are under the curse," in addition reminding us that the "law is not of faith" (Galatians 3:12).[18] Owen says that the law communicates to one and all "do this and live; fail and die."[19] Both in general and in particular, the law pronounces sentence with no right of appeal.[20]

---

17. III:429.
18. VI:389.
19. VI:389.
20. VI:389.

The Function of the Law Positively Defined

The Law is "Connatural" to the Sinner

Owen uses the term "connatural" to describe the proximity of God's law to every sinner ("domestic" and "acquaintance" are synonymous with "connatural"). He contends that the law of God and the sinner are companions,[21] in Owen's mind inseparable from birth:

> It came into the world with him, and hath grown up with him from his infancy. It was implanted in his heart by nature,—is his own reason; he can never shake it off or part with it. It is his familiar, his friend, that cleaves to him as the flesh to the bone; so that they who have not the law written cannot but show forth the work of the law . . . because the law itself is inbred to them. And all the faculties of the soul are at peace with it, in subjection to it. It is the bond and ligament of their union, harmony, and correspondency among themselves, in all their moral actings. It gives life, order, motion to them all.[22]

Because an everlasting union embeds a sinner in God's law, Owen argues that the sinner ought to heed the testimony that the law represents:[23]

> Now, shall not a man rather believe a domestic, a friend, indeed himself, than a foreigner, as stranger, that comes with uncouth principles, and such a suit is not reason at all? 1 Corinthians 1:18.[24]

Natural law coexists with sinners, compelling the conscience to condemn sinful acts.[25]

---

21. VI:389.
22. VI. 390.
23. VI. 390.
24. VI:390.
25. VI:390.

The Law and Conscience Concur in Their Communication to the Sinner

The concurrence of testimony linking law and conscience is constant, says Owen, interpreting Romans 1:32 in this light. Should the law say, "this or that is a sin worthy of death" our conscience replies, "It is even so," and then continues, "This and that is sin, so worthy of death, is the soul guilty of." The law replies, "Then die as thou hast deserved,"[26] and pronounces the sinner dead.

The Law Receives Concurrence from the Sinner

The law's message to the soul is "against the soul's interest," asserts Owen. But because the law communicates only justice, righteousness, and equity, the law is persuasive enough to gain the soul's consent.[27] Citing Romans 1:32, Owen reminds us that all men know that the voice of the law is the "judgment of God," confirmation for which is in Romans 7:12–13, "wherefore the law is holy, and the commandment holy, and just, and good. Was then that which was good made death unto me? God forbid. But sin, that it might appear sin, working death in me by that which is good; that sin by the commandment might become exceeding sinful." It is the authority of the law, the way it accords with conscience, and the reasonableness of the things it proposes, that convinces us of its veracity.[28]

The Law Speaks with Authority

To disbelieve the law, according to Owen, is to call God a liar. When the law speaks, it speaks not in its own name but in the name of the one who has authored it. Owen sees the commonality

---

26. VI:390.
27. VI:390.
28. VI:390.

shared by law and God's substance as an important connection,[29] adding authority to the demands of the law.

The Law Contradicts False Notions of Forgiveness

Owen says categorically that testimony ascribed to the law is such that there is no forgiveness, asserting further that "they that shall flatter themselves with a contrary persuasion will find themselves woefully mistaken at the great day."[30] According to Owen, even the heathen philosophers understand that God is the avenger, and that it is his province as ruler and governor of the universe to exact punishment for all sin.[31] Using as his example a heathen's fear of God's judgment, Owen asserts that such people tremble with fear in the presence of "thunderings, lightnings, tempests, or darkness." The heathen's secret belief is that God is nigh, and a consuming fire.[32] The universal belief that there is a God, and that He is the avenger of sin, mitigates any false hopes of remission.[33]

Owen's View of the Limitations of the Law of God

Although Owen validates and defines the grandeur and breadth of the law, he does not see the law as a self-sufficient means of recognizing sin. The mirror is accurate, but the sinner does not have eyes to see what is truly reflected. A sinner lacks the wherewithal to recognize the sin, and because of this inability to perceive and utilize spiritual truth, Christ sends his Spirit to convince the world of its sin (John 16:8).[34]

---

29. VI:391–92.
30. VI:391.
31. VI:392.
32. VI:392.
33. VI:392.
34. II:95.

OWEN'S EXPOSITION OF THE LAW OF GOD IN PARTICULAR

God Is the Sovereign Lawgiver

In his discussion of James 4:12, "There is one lawgiver, who is able to save and to destroy," Owen highlights the sovereignty of the sole Lawgiver. God alone has power to prescribe whatever laws he pleases.[35] Owen explains that when orders come from one who himself has a superior, then the order has limited credibility, because the superior might choose to countermand it. As Owen says: "there is no room for tergiversation"[36] so that when God's orders are disobeyed, we may infer that person is despised, for to disobey his commands is to despise the "whole authority of God."[37] The Scriptures remind us that God refers to sinners who break his commands as "despising of him" (Numbers 11:20; 1 Samuel 2:30), "despising of his name" (Malachi 1:6), and the "despising of his commandment" (2 Samuel 12:9).[38] Owen concludes: "Being, then, under the command of God to be holy, not to endeavor always and in all things so to be is to despise God, to reject his sovereign authority over us, and to live in defiance of him."[39]

The General Distinctions of the Moral Law, Ceremonial Law, and the Law of Christ

Owen believes that it is necessary to make distinctions regarding the Old Testament law, and that these are twofold—moral and ceremonial, and not threefold (moral, judicial, and ceremonial), the categories common to Reformed circles of our own times.[40] Owen

---

35. III:610.
36. III:610.
37. III:610.
38. III:610.
39. III:610.
40. V:30.

grouped the Decalogue, the case laws, and the sanctions appended to the case laws into a single category, "the moral law."

The Laws of Christ Are Executed by His Apostles

In Owen's view the Apostles have the authority to execute all of Christ's laws, "with the penalties annexed unto their disobedience," citing 2 Corinthians 10:6: "We have in a readiness wherewith to revenge all disobedience." The punishment for disobedience is excommunication, in the main. He defines excommunication as the "judiciary excision of any person or persons from the society of the faithful and visible body of Christ in the world."[41]

The New Testament Believer's Liberty from the Law

The New Testament Believer's Liberty from the Ceremonial Law

As with other Protestants, Owen agrees that the Old Testament ceremonial ordinances are no longer binding upon believers, who are freed from the law of ordinances. (According to the Jerusalem general assembly, this was the burden that believers of Old Testament times could not carry, Acts 15:10). Owen sees a link between Colossians 2:14 and Galatians 5:1, in relation to Old Testament ceremonial law. Owen interprets Colossians 2:14, as do most Reformation Protestants, to mean that Christ refuted ceremonial elements of the law, thus "taking them out of the way" by "nailing them to his cross." Believers must therefore "stand fast in the liberty wherewith Christ hath made us free" (Galatians 5:1). Christ's abrogation of ceremonial ordinances leaves those who follow New Testament teachings at liberty to do so.[42]

---

41. IV:444.
42. II:212.

The New Testament Believer's Liberty from the Terror of the Moral Law

Owen sees that not only is a person who believes in the New Testament freed from Old Testament ceremonial law, but also he can enjoy certain liberties regarding moral law. In Owen's opinion, Old Testament moral law is "rigorous," resulting in "terror," alluding to God's giving the law to Moses on Mount Sinai (Exodus 19 and 20). The "dread and terror" of that occasion is absent from the New Testament, where a sense of freedom prevails because people are compelled by dread and terror no longer.[43] Owen cites in evidence Hebrews 12:18–22, "we are not come to the mount that might be touched, and that burned with fire, to the whirlwind, darkness, and tempest, to the sound of the trumpet, and the voice of words, which they that heard besought that they might hear it no more; but we are come to mount Sion . . ."

The New Testament Believer's Liberty from the Impossibility of Accomplishing Moral Law

For Owen the New Testament believer also lives in a state of relative liberty from the impositions of moral law. Because of Christ's ministry, such believers find themselves exempted from having to merit salvation by obeying the law. Owen regards this liberty as one of the blessings of the New Testament, as subscribed to in Romans 8:2–3 and Galatians 3:21–23. The righteousness of Christ relieves believers from their debt to moral law (Romans 8:3). These believers are enabled to meet the demands of law by the Spirit. It is the Spirit that energizes New Testament believers to live out the righteousness of Christ, who lives within them.[44]

---

43. II:212.
44. II:212.

JOHN OWEN'S VIEW OF SUBSTANTIVE BIBLICAL LAW

The New Testament Believer's Liberty from the Results of Transgression of the Moral Law

Owen contends that there are two outcomes of moral law that afflict every transgressor, and these are either a curse or death.[45] "The whole wrath annexed" to moral law constitutes a curse. Galatians 3:3 establishes that a believer is delivered from the curse: "Christ hath redeemed us from the curse of the law by being made a curse for us."[46] Not only is the believer redeemed from the curse of the law but also from the sentence of the law, which is death itself. (According to Hebrews 2:15, the New Testament believer is at liberty from death.)[47]

The New Testament Believer's Liberty from Satan, Sin, the World, and the Claims of Satan, Sin, and the World

Additionally, the liberty of the New Testament believer excludes the influence of Satan (Hebrews 2:14 and Colossians 1:13).[48] This is a liberty from sin (Romans 6:14 and 1 Peter 1:18).[49] Moreover, not only is the New Testament believer set at liberty from the world (Galatians 1:4)[50] but also is free from "all the attendancies, advantages, and claims" of Satan, sin, and the world (Galatians 4:3-5 and Colossians 2:20).

---

45. II:212.
46. II:212.
47. II:212.
48. II:212.
49. II:212.
50. II:212.

The Relation of Christ to the Law of God

The Ceremonial Law of the Old Testament Represented the Glory of Christ

Extolling the virtues of Old Testament ceremonial law, Owen remarks:

> What were the tabernacle and temple? What was the holy place with the utensils of it? What was the oracle, the ark, the cherubim, the mercy-seat, placed therein? What was the high priest in all his vestments and administrations? What were the sacrifices and annual sprinkling of blood in the most holy place? What was the whole system of their religious worship? Were they anything but representations of Christ in the glory of his person and his office? They were a shadow, and the body represented by that shadow was Christ.[51]

In his treatment of Hebrews 9, Owen says: "all that Moses did in the erection of the tabernacle, and the institution of all its services, was but to give antecedent testimony by way of representation, unto the things of Christ that were afterward to be revealed." This was the substance of the prophets' ministry (1 Peter 1:11–12)[52] hence Owen calls ceremonial laws "the dark apprehensions of the glory of Christ," and therefore "the life of the church of old."[53]

Christ Declared the Spiritual Inward Nature of the Law of God

In his discussion of Christ's relation to the law, Owen points out that the Jews entertained a belief that the law would reclaim its former purity when the Messiah came. For this reason, Owen highlights the importance of the law in Christ's ministry:

> Herein did the Lord Christ place the beginning of his prophetical office and ministry, Matthew 5, 6, 7. He

---

51. I:348.
52. I:348, 49.
53. I:349.

opened, unveiled, explained, and vindicated, the preceptive part of the will of God before revealed, to the end that by a compliance therewith we should be holy.

Christ revealed the inward spiritual nature of the law, the truth of its interpretation, "their nature, signification, and extent, vindicating them from all the corrupt and false glosses which passed current in the church, whereby there was an abatement made of their efficacy and an indulgence granted unto the lusts of men."[54] Making his point, he draws on an example that Christ himself acknowledged. At the time of Christ, biblical scholars insisted that "thou shalt not kill" referred only to murder.[55] Christ, as the Great Prophet, explained how the commandment forbad injurious thoughts as well, thus reviving the truth of the law.

Christ Is Not a Lawgiver of a New Law

Long before the ministry of J.N. Darby, founder of the Plymouth Brethren and the dispensational hermeneutic, a debate raged even in the Puritan era regarding whether Christ instituted laws or merely endorsed those that existed already. Richard Baxter, for instance, the chief proponent of "neo-nomianism," held that Christ instituted a new law, which if a sinner obeyed, would result in salvation. In dealing with this very issue, Owen says he will not "inmix" himself "in any needless disputations," but in his catechism contends that Christ endorsed laws existing at the Creation and codified on Mount Horeb. Owen would not endorse neo-nomianism. Were he privy to the modern debate over dispensationalism, Owen would not endorse Darby's point of view.[56]

For him Old Testament law divides into two: the moral preceptive category and the category of institutional worship, both of

---

54. III:632.
55. III:632.
56. III:632.

which Owen regarded as law;[57] any part not included in institutional worship he describes as "moral."

Owen is adamantly against what is now called the dispensational hermeneutic, particularly in relation to the moral preceptive category of Old Testament law:

> The Lord Christ gave no new law, nor was the old abrogated by him—which it must be if another were given in the room of it, unto the same ends. For the introduction of a new law in the place of and unto the end of a former, is an actual abrogation of it. Neither did he add any new precepts unto it, nor give any counsels for the performance of duties in matter or manner beyond what it prescribed.[58]

Rebutting what came to be associated with Darby, Owen forwards two propositions: in the first place, any abrogation of old law is "contrary to the wisdom and holiness of God in giving the law," and thus is both unwise and unholy. Owen judges as unwise any effort to inaugurate a law, only to abrogate it at a later date, a process that is contradictory: "why do something if you are going to later undo it?"[59] In the second place, Owen sees the making and dismantling as an admission that the law is not holy: "if the law had to be abrogated, the law must be unworthy or inferior." Such a process is "inconsistent with the nature of the law itself," for to abrogate a law is to admit that its nature is imperfect, and since indeed the law is perfect, then it cannot be dismissed.[60] Ceremonial law is transformed, rather than dismissed, according to Owen.

In conclusion Owen states: "Wherefore, no additions were made unto the preceptive part of the law by our Savior, nor counsels given by him for the performance of more than it did require."[61] Moreover, he regards the Gospel as the source "no new law," rejecting Richard Baxter's neo-nomian argument. Owen

57. I:135.
58. I:135.
59. I:135.
60. I:135.
61. I:135.

believes in the "duties of the moral and eternal law as plainly declared in the doctrine" of the Gospel, but refutes the notion that these are newly inaugurated, since Gospel law is "enforced in the motives." Christ is not a new lawgiver: "Nor in this sense did the Lord Christ ever declare himself to be a new lawgiver; yea, he declares the contrary—that he came to confirm the old, Matthew 5:17."[62] For Owen, this connection proves that any moral and preceptive part of the Old Testament has abiding validity.

Making his case, Owen asserts that 1 John 2:7-8 affirms Christ's "new commandment" of love, by establishing that it is an "old commandment."[63] In contrast, the institutions of worship given to Moses at Mount Horeb included various "statutes and judgments" which were "abolished by Christ."[64] Owen's interpretation of Hebrews 3:3-6 convinces him that the Old Testament institutions of worship were "appointed," but only until "time of reformation."[65] Christ, as the "supreme Lord and lawgiver of the Gospel Church," replaces the old with a new law of worship.

Concerning the New Testament, Owen sees obedience to Christ as twofold: first, obeying Christ is obedience to the moral law, and second, obedience to Christ is obedience to the law of evangelical worship, as instituted by him.[66] Here Owen defines evangelical obedience: "if they intend the duties which the moral law requireth, proceeding from, and performed by, faith in Christ, upon the rounds of the love of God in him, and grace received from him—then they are duties purely evangelical."[67] He distinguishes evangelical obedience from obedience that is only mechanical. Although people cannot deprive the "original power" to inspire universal obedience, this is evangelical in nature, procured for Christians by their "confirmation unto the Evangelical Church."[68]

62. I:135.
63. I:136.
64. I:135.
65. I:135-36.
66. I:135-36.
67. I:136.
68. I:136.

Owen separates mankind into those who receive the Gospel and those who do not. Since God "hath given unto the Lord Christ all power in his name," Christ has the authority to compel evangelical obedience of those who have received the Gospel. Those who have not are "left under the original authority of the Law, either as implanted in our natures at their first creation, as are the Gentiles; or as delivered by Moses, and written in tables of stone, as it was with the Jews" (Romans 2:12–15).[69]

Owen has no hesitation in citing Christ as the Gospel lawgiver:

> But as unto them that are called unto the faith of the Gospel, the authority of Christ doth immediately affect their minds and consciences. 'He feeds' or rules his people 'in the strength of the Lord, in the majesty of the name of the Lord his God,' Micah 5:4. All the authority and majesty of God is in him and with him;—so of old, as the great Angel of God's presence, he was in the church in the wilderness with a delegated power, Exodus 23:20–22. So is he still immediately present with the church, requiring obedience in the name and majesty of God.[70]

Obedience to the One to whom God has imparted ultimate authority over the church is the "way whereby God will be glorified."[71] Owen sees both continuity and discontinuity between law as given to Moses (Galatians 3:19; *cf.* Micah 4:4) and that given to the church through Jesus Christ.[72]

The Old Testament law has "original power" to command obedience because of its "first institution" at the Creation. From this "original power" the Old Testament law has neither lost its validity nor diminished it in any way.[73] Those who follow New Testament law, are obliged, however, to "have respect unto" Old Testament law, even elements of Old Testament law that are "hard

---

69. I:137.
70. I:138.
71. I:138.
72. I:136.
73. I:136

and difficult." Old Testament law "continueth still in its original authority and power, which it had from the beginning," binding believers of New Testament law because the old is continued in the new.[74]

Christ Is the Lawgiver of the Church

The experience of faith, according to Owen, brings the soul into the ambit of Christ's divine authority, an authority so thorough that the soul will come to despise all other things.[75] Christ's authority as the exclusive "great head and lawgiver of the church" entitles Him to institute all worship; in view of this, anyone who imposes on this usurps the crown and dignity of Christ,[76] since only Christ has the power to institute worship in heaven and on earth. Owen argues that if a believer relieves his conscience by impugning the authority of Christ, then he will "find [that] all other authorities... come to nothing."[77]

The Relation of the Law of God to Creation

The Created Law of Operation in All of Creation

According to Owen, all of creation reflects the "law of operation," as embedded by the Creator. This "law of operation" is the ruling principle that determines every act. Everything under Creation acts according to inherent laws of God, laws that determine its existence.[78]

Owen illustrates his argument for a creative implanted law by example: Fire, because of its nature, must ascend, whereas objects containing mass must descend, and water, being fluid in nature,

74. I:137.
75. IX:502.
76. IX:502.
77. IX:502.
78. VI:303, 304.

must flow. If a millstone were to fall, but was caught and hurled upward, the force that converted its direction would be a "matter of wonderful force, power, and efficacy."[79] That which overrules the creative implanted controlling law must itself be considerable.[80]

From this, Owen draws further analogies, in this case regarding sin: sin is also a matter of remarkable force, power, and efficacy, since it impels created man to act in a manner contrary to the creative implanted controlling law.[81] The urge of species to nurture their young is another example of this law.[82] "Concreated" with most creatures is a love for their young. Although most creatures have this "instinct and inclination," Owen recalls the foolish ostrich of Job 39:16–17 which does not conform, but manifests a different implanted law, and mistreats its young.[83]

Developing his argument that sin counteracts the creative implanted controlling law, Owen turns to Romans 1:31,[84] where "without natural affection" invokes the heartlessness of parents who murder their own children, even newborn. The "barbarous custom among the Romans," whereby they avoid the inconvenience of an unhealthy child by destroying them, shows that the Romans could "repel the force and nature" of the law within them, in so doing revealing the strength of sin.[85]

In the same vein, Owen decries abortion, calling it the act of a woman who is murdering her own child. Any reasoning that convinces a woman demonstrates the deceitfulness of sin,[86] for in this act sin turns the "strong current of nature," darkening all the light of God in the soul.[87] Owen alludes to the abomination described in Ezekiel 16:20–21 and Psalm 106:37–38, when parents turn their

79. VI:304.
80. VI:304.
81. VI:304.
82. VI:304.
83. VI:304, 305.
84. VI:304, 305.
85. VI:305.
86. VI:305.
87. VI:305

children to ashes. The idolatrous priests that assisted in this act afforded relief by making "noise and clamor" to drown out the "woeful moans and cries of the poor, dying, tormented infants."[88] The enormity of the parents' sin corrupts the "whole law of their being and dependence upon God."[89] To these examples Owen adds the murder of children by their parents, murdering one's spouse, sodomy, incest, the murder of Abel, the treason of Judas, and the villainy of Nero, all of them rebellion against the prime dictates of the law of nature.[90]

The Created Law and Light of Nature

Owen holds that the "law and light of nature" is embedded in every one of us. His interpretation of Romans 1:19 and 2:14–15 says that the consecrated law and light of nature in each human enables that person to make a judgment between good and evil actions. Because of this inward law and light of nature, all are under an obligation to obedience.[91]

The Law of God Written in the Heart

According to Owen, God does not put his law into a heart that is incapable of obedience, for God says, "I will put a new spirit within them," implying there are no inhibiting conditions. Just as the God of the Old Covenant wrote on the tablets of stone, in the New Covenant he writes on the heart. Owen emphasizes that the principle of obedience is "actually wrought of God in us,"[92] in reference to its precise nature adding, "The end of the work of God described is

---

88. VI:306.
89. VI:306.
90. VI:306.
91. III:278.
92. III:328.

not a power to obey, which may be exerted or not; but it is actual obedience in conversion, and the fruits of it."[93]

The writing of God's law on the heart is according to a promise made in Jeremiah 31:28-34:

> And if God do not in these promises declare a real efficiency of internal grace, taking away all repugnancy of nature unto conversion, curing its depravation actually and effectually, and communicating infallibly a principle of scriptural obedience, I know not in what words such a work may be expressed.[94]

Prayer Is a Duty of the Law of Nature

For Owen the forms of prayer are not an institution of the covenant of works or the covenant of grace; rather, prayer is law of nature:

> Prayer itself is a duty of the law of nature, and being of such singular and indispensable use unto all persons, the commands for it are reiterated in the Scripture beyond those concerning any other particular duty whatever; and if it hath respect unto Jesus Christ, with sundry ordinances of the gospel to be performed in this name, it falls under a new divine institution.[95]

Part of the New Covenant, the 'new divine institution,' is comprised of the many commands regarding prayer in the New Testament.[96]

---

93. III:328.
94. III:328.
95. IV:341.
96. IV:341-42.

John Owen's View of Substantive Biblical Law

The Relation of the Law of God to Sin

Indwelling Sin Is a Law

The introduction to Owen's thesis that sin is a law is drawn from the Apostle Paul's confession (Romans 6), "I find a law." Paul described his sinful nature as a "law" because this nature has power; and it has efficacy—"where there is a law there is power."[97] According to Owen, all laws have two attendant characteristics: on the one hand, a law has dominion or power and on the other, efficacy.[98]

He turns to Romans 7:1 to describe the dominion function of the law of sin: "the law hath dominion over a man whilst he liveth," choosing the Greek version of "hath dominion" (κυριεύει) to demonstrate that, by its very nature, a law "plays the part of a superior." Claiming that its nature is to exact obedience,[99] Owen argues that dominion is a function of a law (Romans 6:12, βασιλευέτω, "to reign as a king," and 7:1, κυριεύει, "to lord it.")[100] Dominion (the κυριεύει of Romans 7:1) has a dual nature, moral authority and real efficacy. A law has moral authority over a man and real efficacy also.[101]

While for an unbeliever, the moral authority of the law of sin is complete and unchallenged, the believer, on the other hand, experiences the moral authority of the law of sin as still present but broken and severely weakened. Though the law of sin residing within believers is weakened, it is not changed. The real efficacy of a law is its capability of provoking "those that are obnoxious unto it unto the things that it requireth."[102] Thus, in order to provoke the obnoxious to obey, a law has rewards and punishments. All laws

---

97. VI:165.
98. VI:165.
99. VI:163.
100. VI:163.
101. VI:163–64.
102. VI:164.

maintain an efficacy, says Owen, "from the rewards and punishments that are annexed unto them."[103]

He illustrates the inner conflict of sanctification by reference to Moses,[104] since in him the law of sin and the law of grace conflicted because the rewards of the law of sin were its pleasures. Most people must lose their souls to gain them afresh. In the case of Moses, he submitted to the law of grace, abrogating the law of sin within (Hebrews 11:25–26): "he chose rather to suffer affliction with the people of God, than to enjoy the pleasures of sin for a season; for he looked unto the recompense of reward." Moses sought the reward of the law of grace but was caught in the horns of a dilemma: on the one hand, he sinned at the expense of his soul, on the other, the reward of grace would cost him enjoyment of his sins.[105]

The law of sin rules the world at large,[106] where those who would cast it amok, though fear it still, cannot inherit the kingdom of God (Revelation 21:8, the fearful shall have no share in eternal life). The law of sin punishes those who would escape its influence. It shapes the character and conduct by threatening sins of commission and omission.[107]

Of punishments merited by the law of sin, Owen states: "It hath also punishments that it threatens men with who labor to cast off its yoke. What ever evil, trouble, or danger in the world, attends gospel obedience,—whatever hardship of violence to be offered to the sensual part of our natures in a strict course of mortification—sin makes use of, as if they were punishments attending the neglect of its commands."[108] Where loss of prestige, power, or position affects sinners, and the pleasures of sin are lost to them, then it is the law of sin that has brought about this downfall.[109]

103. VI:164.
104. VI:164.
105. VI:164.
106. VI:164.
107. VI:164.
108. VI:164.
109. VI:165.

The law of sin can affect even believers, Owen adds,[110] since believers must be prepared to reject inducements to sin, without which "there is no standing before the power of the law."[111] To Owen, the law of sin is not an "outward, written, commanding, directing law, but an inbred, working, impelling, urging law."[112]

Owen distinguishes the nature of an inbred law from an externally proposed law. Before his fall, Adam was implicated in an externally proposed law that came from Eve. Having no inbred tendency against this overture of sin, he could have withstood its temptation. An inbred law affects thoughts and actions,[113] because its "inbred" dimension appearing in the original created state of mankind, according to Owen, in the created state of man, the law of God was inbred and natural. The law of God was "concreated with his faculties, and was their rectitude, both in being and operation, in reference to his end of living unto God and glorifying Him."[114] For Adam obeying God was easy and pleasant, because before the fall his heart knew the inbred law of God; his God gave an "especial power in the whole soul to enable it unto all obedience."[115]

Although our constitution has been altered by sin so that the law of God is now "by nature cast out of the soul," Owen believes something of the original constitution remains. After the fall, people retained some components of the pure original. Since the original law of God is inbred, it is "powerful and effective"—and its remaining vestiges remain powerful and effective in the conscience of the sinner (Romans 2:14–15).

Owen understands that God writes the law of God upon the hearts of the newly converted, sanctifying them by writing his law upon their hearts, a practice that Owen rejoices.[116] God knows he

110. VI:165.
111. VI:165.
112. VI:165.
113. VI:165.
114. VI:165.
115. VI:165.
116. VI:165, 166.

must implant his law, in this manner, in order to regenerate the sinner[117]:

> I will put my law in their inward parts, and write it in their hearts. The written law will not do it: mercies and deliverances from distress will not effect it; trials and afflictions will not accomplish it. Then will I take another course; I will turn the written law into an internal living principle in their hearts; and that will have such an efficacy as shall assuredly make them my people, and keep them so.[118]

People must find out that an external outward law is insufficient to lead men them obedience.[119] Further, because sin is the inward controlling principle in an unbeliever's heart, God implants a more powerful principle. Owen describes indwelling sin as not only a law but also as an inward habit,[120] one that prompts certain patterns of thought and behavior. Since indwelling sin repeatedly directs, inclines, and moves one to patterns of behavior, an inward law of grace must.

The inwardness of sin affords its various advantages, since inwardness increases its strength and furthers its causes. In the first place, sin is ever-present in the soul.[121] (Sin always abides in the soul; "it is never absent.")[122] It is constant, always inhabiting the soul.[123] Thus, there is no respite from sin's claims, at any time; if indeed sin were transient, then we would be more obedient, greatly so.[124]

Owen highlights the constancy of sin by comparing it to the occupation of a walled city. If the city fathers knew when the enemy forces would be absent, they could fortify it during a respite.

117. VI:166.
118. VI:166.
119. VI:166.
120. VI:166.
121. VI:166.
122. VI:166.
123. VI:166.
124. VI:166.

However, in our case, the home of sin is the soul: "there it dwells, and is no wanderer." Sin is a like burning coal continually in our houses; "which, if it be not looked unto, will fire them, and it may consume them."¹²⁵

Next Owen develops further his idea that sin is a constant presence in the soul:

> Wherever you are, whatever you are about, this law of sin is always in you; in the best that you do, and in the worst. Men little consider what a dangerous companion is always at home with them. When they are in company, when alone, by night or by day, all is one sin is with them ... Oh, the woeful security of poor souls! How little do the most of men think of this inbred enemy that is never far from home! How little, for the most part, doth the watchfulness of any professors answer the danger of their state and condition!

Secondly, sin also increases its strength and furthers its causes because it is "ready to apply itself to every end and purpose that is serves unto." Owen cites as his example the testimony of the Apostle Paul: "it doth not only dwell in me, but when I would do good, it is present with me."¹²⁶

In other words, says Owen: "An inmate may dwell in a house, and yet not be always meddling with what the good-man of the house hath to do (that so we may keep to the allusion of indwelling, used by the Apostle): but it is so with this law, it doth so dwell in us, as that it will be present within everything we do."¹²⁷ According to Owen, when we would do good, the evil within us is more active; "Would you pray, would you hear, would you give alms, would you meditate, would you be in any duty acting faith on God and love towards him, would you work righteousness, would you resist temptations—this troublesome, perplexing indweller will still more or less put itself upon you and be present with you; so that you cannot perfectly and completely accomplish the thing that is

---

125. VI:166.
126. VI:167.
127. VI:167.

good." The law of indwelling sin affects us, because our minds are given to "darkness and vanity," our affections to "sensuality," and our wills to "a loathing of and aversion from that which is good."[128] Sin continually compels us with its "inclinations, motions, or suggestions to evil," affecting us most when we are inclined to do good.[129]

Thirdly, Owen states that the law of sin applies itself to our work with great facility (Hebrews 12:1): "it needs no doors to be opened unto it" and "it needs no engines to work by,"[130] affecting every part of our constitution. If we apply ourselves, sin affects us with ignorance, darkness, vanity, folly, and madness. If our hearts are affectionate, sin acts on it by "inclinations to the world and present things, and sensuality, with proneness to all manner of defilements." Sin affects our entire constitution, even to possessing the "very faculties of the soul whereby we must do what we do."[131]

Owen describes the estate of the masses as pitiful. Sin is so exacting and pervasive that humanity is ignorant of its hold on them. Under its dominion, they are blinded from seeing its implications by the act of domination[132]:

> They find not that there is darkness and folly in their minds; because they are darkness itself, and darkness will discover nothing. They find not deadness and an indisposition in their hearts and wills to God, because they are dead wholly in trespasses and sins. They are at peace with their lusts, by being in bondage unto them. And this is the state of most men in the world; which makes them woefully despise all their eternal concernments.[133]

---

128. VI:167.
129. VI:167.
130. VI:167.
131. VI:167.
132. VI:168.
133. VI:168.

JOHN OWEN'S VIEW OF SUBSTANTIVE BIBLICAL LAW

The Knowledge of Sin Is by the Law

The Function of the Law in General

Summarizing his understanding of law itself, Owen discusses "Communion with the Son Jesus Christ"; the reason for this law has to do with transgression (Romans 7:12 and Galatians 3:19). The law was given because of human sin (causal), and to revive the good and evil of man at Creation (doctrinal). The law restores to us what original sin damaged. The law serves as a mirror at which one may look and perceive sin "in all its ugliness and deformity."[134]

Further summarizing the content, manner of delivery, sanctions, and function of law, Owen asserts that it is characterized by "purity, holiness, compass, and perfection."[135] It was delivered amid "dread, terror, thunder, earthquakes, and fire" (Exodus 19:18–20, Deuteronomy 4:11, and Hebrews 12:18–21),[136] its sanctions including "death, curse, and wrath."[137] The function is to make a "wonderful discovery" of sin, because "upon every account [its] "pollution, guilt, and exceeding sinfulness" are exposed by the law.[138]

Sin Works Violence to the Law of Nature Implanted in Mankind

Owen believes that sin manifests its power in the unregenerate, such that were an observer to document this power, he need only record the nature of the sins committed.[139] This record of the sins of the will have a salutary effect on believers, who must look to their own, understand how easily might these sins grow and fructify.[140] Owen explains: "believers may be taught what is the power and

---

134. II:95.
135. II:95.
136. II:95.
137. II:95.
138. II:94–95.
139. VI:303.
140. VI:303.

efficacy of that plague of sin which is in and among them by the effects the same plague produceth in and among others, who have not those corrections of its poison and those preservatives from death which the Lord Jesus Christ hath furnished them withal."[141] Referring to Psalm 106:37–38 and Ezekiel 16:20–21, he remains:

> They took their children and burnt them to ashes in a soft fire; the wicked priests that assisted in the sacrifice affording them this relief, that they made a noise and clamor that the vile wretches might not hear the woeful moans and cries of the poor, dying tormented infants.[142]

Guilt Is the Law Voicing Its Objection to Sin

Here is Owen on the voice of conscience, which is a natural law, written upon the heart:

> Conscience, if not seared, inexorably condemneth and pronounceth wrath and anger upon the soul that hath the least guilt cleaving to it. Now, it hath this advantage, it lieth close to the soul, and by importunity and loud speaking it will be heard in what it hath to say; it will make the whole soul attend, or it will speak like thunder. And its constant voice is, that where there is guilt there must be judgment.[143]

(His discussion of natural law in the human heart is drawn from Romans 2:14–15.)[144]

The Content of Biblical Law Opposes Sin

Biblical law opposes sin in several ways, the first way being that it exposes sin, by discovering it:[145]

141. VI:303
142. VI:306.
143. VI:387.
144. VI:387.
145. VI:313.

> The measure of the strength of any person or defenced city may be well taken from the opposition that they are able to withstand and not be prevailed against. If we hear of a city that has endured a long siege from a potent enemy, and yet is not taken or conquered, whose will have endured great batteries and are not demolished, though we have never seen the place, yet we conclude it strong, if not impregnable.[146]

Although the law exposes and condemns it, sin is "able to hold out," and not only to survive, but to "secure its reign and dominion." Despite the law's strength, sin maintains itself in stubborn resistance to it, in this respect constant, in character volatile, being both great and terrible.[147] The resistance of sin to the law is always fruitless, however, because sin can do no good.[148]

The purpose of biblical law is to "discover the enemy; it convinceth the soul that there is a such a traitor harbouring in its bosom,"[149] just as a physician exposes an unknown disease. Since most people have no idea that they are diseased by sin, the law serves as a means of diagnosing its presence.[150] Owen sees biblical law as the soldier who discovers an enemy within the city walls. The law is a seeker so, searching for sin, it is exposed once and for all.[151] In Romans 6, Paul testifies that "I had not known sin," an admission that he was not aware of the dominion and power of sin, a phrase that Owen interprets relatively. He believes that when a Pharisee, Paul was not absolutely ignorant of his sinful nature, but rather he was relatively ignorant of it. Hence, Paul did not know his sin nature "fully, clearly, distinctly."[152] Examining people's understanding of sin, Owen sees their consciences as inferior expressions of their moral selves. Conscience is barely audible as a

---

146. VI:313.
147. VI:313.
148. VI:313.
149. VI:313.
150. VI:313.
151. VI:313.
152. VI:313.

reminder of laws written on the heart, for (*cf.* John 1:5) conscience "gives a man such a sight of it as the blind man had in the gospel upon the first touch of his eyes." The blind man could see "obscurely" and "confusedly,"[153] as his sight returned:

> This, then, the law doth—it draws out this traitor from secret lurking places, the intimate recesses of the soul. A man, when the law comes, is no more ignorant of his enemy. If he will now perish by him, it is openly and knowingly; he cannot but say that the law warned him of him, discovered him unto him, yea, and raised a concourse about his sin in the soul of various affections, as an officer doth that discovers a thief or robber, calling out for assistance to apprehend him."[154]

Because of the law, a sinner cannot regard sin a trifling matter,[155] for the sinner is made to see the sins of his own soul, including its vileness, abomination, enmity to God, and God's hatred of it[156]:

> As a man finds himself somewhat distempered, sending for a physician of skill, when he comes requires his judgment of this distemper; he, considering his condition, tells him, 'Alas! I am sorry for you; the case is far otherwise with you than you imagine: your disease is mortal, and it hath proceeded so far, pressing upon your spirits and infecting the whole mass of your blood, that I doubt, unless most effectual remedies be used, you will live but a very few hours."

The sinner's awakening to the nature and extent of his sin happens in stages. First, his conscience (which includes the moral law that God has written upon the heart), may trouble him, and he "finds all not so well as it should be with him, more from the effects of sin and its continual eruptions than the nature of it, which

---

153. VI:314.
154. VI:314.
155. VI:314.
156. VI:314.

he hopes to wrestle withal."[157] The world's false religions remain at this stage, since most have only a rude, indistinct, and incomplete conception of sin. On the other hand, biblical religion, which includes biblical law, leads the sinner into a second stage of spiritual and epistemological self-consciousness. In the next place, the law responds to sin[158] by communicating to the soul that sin is a disease that is "deadly and mortal, that it is exceeding sinful, as being the root and cause of all his alienation from God."[159]

Owen explains further the function of law in relation to judging people, since it explains what the sinner should expect. In this respect, the law has an illuminating function, a "discovery property," that prepares the sinner for judgment. This offers a sinner fair notice of the judgment, and is evidence of God's justice. For Owen the law of God is oracular, since it personally pleads with sinners: "Thou art the 'man' in whom this exceeding sinful sin doth dwell, and you must answer for the guilt of it."[160]

Owen says that when the law becomes the oracle that voices divine wrath, an unrepentant sinner will "rouse up" in antagonism to the law: "... this, methinks, if anything, should rouse up a man to set himself in opposition to it, yea, utterly to destroy it."[161] On this point the law is unequivocal: "Abide in this state and perish." According to Owen "God serves warrant on all sinners, first of all in warning, giving notice of God's wrath, and secondly, notice that the sin is inexcusable." The first pertains to the wages of sin in the world of the sinner; the second to God's justice in the world to come.[162]

Furthering his examination of law, Owen describes it as disquieting the soul, affrighting the soul, and even killing it. Owen means that the law does not allow the sinner to "enjoy the least

---

157. VI:314.
158. VI:314, 15.
159. VI:314-315.
160. VI:315.
161. VI:315.
162. VI:315.

rest or quietness in harboring its sinful inmate,"¹⁶³ since the law makes the soul "quake and tremble" immediately when one sins, just as if sinners were beasts with a fatal arrow stuck in their sides. Wherever the beast goes thereafter, the arrow does its work.¹⁶⁴

Owen says the law causes the death of the soul, for although a sinner may try to find comfort in self-righteousness and vain hope, these ineffective remedies leave the offender "poor, dead, helpless, and hopeless." Interpreting Romans 7:9, Owen argues that the law convinces the sinner that his sin merits punishment by alluding to the story of a warrior who was born of the earth. Felled in a battle, he would rise again from the earth to fight on, with renewed vigor. So too with sin, which rises again and again until by force it overpowers the soul, forcing it to admit that it deserves to be judged.¹⁶⁵ Hence, the law "slays" sin.¹⁶⁶

Although law demolishes sin, it cannot conquer it, since that is not the law's function. Conquest itself has two aspects, implying both a loss of dominion and strength. Owen makes this point with reference to Christ's parable in Matthew—if one wishes to take the goods of a strong man, then one must first constrain him. The assaults of the law cannot conquer sin in this way, however. Owen interprets Romans 6:3 to mean that the law cannot destroy it to a point where it loses even "one jot of its power and dominion," because a person who "is under the law is also under sin."¹⁶⁷

Owen compares the response of sin to the law to Pharaoh's response to Moses when he demanded freedom for the children of Israel (Exodus 5:19, "they found that they were in a very evil case.") "Finding its rule disturbed, [sin] grows more outrageously oppressive, and doubles the bondage of their souls," a practice it shares with Pharaoh. Owen cites in evidence Romans 7:9-13: "The whole work of the law doth only provoke and enrage sin, and cause it, as it hath opportunity, to put out its strength with more power,

---

163. VI:315.
164. VI:315.
165. VI:315.
166. VI:315.
167. VI:316.

and vigour, and force than formerly."[168] Owen believes that the law aggravates sin, yes, but agrees that preaching the law, even without grace, does result in the relinquishment of many sins and the amendment of lives. He concedes that the power of God's law is such as to limit sin, though it is not designed to subdue it; this is no dishonor because subduing sin is "not its proper work" (Romans 8:3).[169]

Some refrain from sin through the preaching of the law, even if they do so without grace, but most are unmoved by such preaching. Congregations are full of those who remain "deaf, ignorant, senseless, secure, as if they had never been told of the guilt of sin or terror of the Lord."[170]

The Law Gives No Strength Against Sin

Owen contrasts the dominion of grace and the dominion of law,[171] for to be under the dominion of the latter is to be under sin's dominion, since the law cannot subdue sin.[172] "Sin will neither be cast nor kept out of its throne, but by a spiritual power and strength in the soul to oppose, conquer, and dethrone it. Where it is not conquered it will reign; and conquered it will not be without a mighty prevailing power: this the law will not, cannot give."[173]

Citing Romans 6:14 ("not under law, but under grace") Owen categorizes the law accordingly: law is "the whole revelation of the mind and will of God in the Old Testament." In this sense, grace is certainly included in "law." [This meaning is appropriate to an interpretation of Psalm 19:7–9; not only does it contain the law of precepts, but also the promise, and the covenant. It is by means of this promise and covenant that God conveys spiritual strength

---

168. VI:316.
169. VI:316.
170. VI:317.
171. VII:542–44.
172. VII:544.
173. VII:542.

to the church of the Old Testament.]¹⁷⁴ Owen does not interpret the "law" as represented by Romans 6:14 in this sense, however. Rather, he sees law as meaning the covenant of obedience: "Do this, and live." Those under the law are therefore under its "power, rule, conditions, and authority as a covenant."¹⁷⁵

Owen's interpretation of "law" accords with the Cocceius' model of Scripture interpretation. Either one is subject to the law as a covenant of works, or one is subject to grace, as per a covenant of grace. The former maintained Adam before the fall; the law describes the state of those who are fallen.¹⁷⁶ The law was "never ordained of God to convey grace or spiritual strength," says Owen, defining its limitations. If the law could have given life, then righteousness would have come through it, rather than through Christ (Galatians 3:21). The law is not "God's ordinance for the dethroning of sin nor the destruction of its dominion," asserts Owen, because the law does not have "power to bar the entrance of sin, nor to cast it out when it is once enthroned."¹⁷⁷ In sum, the law has "nothing to do with sinners" except "judge, curse, and condemn."¹⁷⁸ The laws of Sinai, added to "its original constitution," are designed to encourage in men a belief in the coming Messiah.¹⁷⁹

1 Corinthians 15:56 says "the strength of sin is the law," which Owen interprets: "The commandment comes home to them, sin reviveth, and they die [Romans 7:9–10]; that is, it gives power to sin to slay the hopes of the sinner, and to distress him the apprehension of guilt and death."¹⁸⁰ In distinguishing the vast differences between law and grace, Owen notices that law gives no liberty of any kind; in contrast, grace delivers into a "liberty of state and condition" and a liberty of "internal operation."¹⁸¹ (The former Owen

---

174. VII:542.
175. VII:543.
176. VII:542–43.
177. VII:543.
178. VII:543.
179. VII:543.
180. VII:543.
181. VII:543.

The Relation of the Law of God to the Gospel

The Order and Use of Law and Gospel

Owen sees the relation of the law to the Gospel as dependent upon the use of the law[183]:

> For that which any man hath first to deal withal, with respect unto his eternal condition, both naturally and by God's institution, is the law. This is first presented unto the soul with its terms of righteousness and life, and with its curse in case of failure. Without this the gospel cannot be understood, nor the grace of it duly valued.[184]

It is indispensable to one's understanding of the Gospel:

> For it [the Gospel] is the revelation of God's way for relieving the souls of men from the sentence and curse of the law, Romans I:17."[185]

The Law's Instrumentality in Conversion

The "efficient cause" of conversion is the Holy Ghost, the agent of which is word of God. For Owen, the law of God as contained by his word is the very agent by which the Holy Spirit effects conversions.[186] For conversion to occur, one must understand the nature, guilt, and curse of sin. It is "from the law of God" that we discover that "afflictions, dangers, sicknesses, fears, and disappointments" may be the Holy Spirit's way to "excite, stir, and put an edge upon

---

182. VII:543.
183. V:75.
184. V:75.
185. V:75.
186. III.351.

the minds and affections of men." The Holy Spirit is the center of conversion, for God Himself is the force of conversion, in order to "reprove men, and set their sins in order before their eyes" (Psalm 50:21). Apart from the work of the Spirit (John 16:8), Owen holds that sinners may hear the law preached every day of their lives and not be once affected by it.[187]

The Relation of the Law of God to Mankind in General

Why Human Laws Are Often Little Respected

Owen explains why human laws are so little respected. Men who transgress weigh the cost against likely punishments. Moreover, he surmises men realize that since lawmakers cannot prosecute penalties in cases of transgression, they need not respect the laws that would inhibit them. Left without effective sanctions, men choose to de-authorize law.[188]

God's law cannot be disdained, however, "without the highest folly and villainy," reminding us that rewards and punishments of God are eternal. There is no room for "mutability, indifferency, ignorance, impotency, or any other pretence that they shall not be executed."[189] God's attributes are "immutably engaged" by applying sanctions inherent to law.[190] If we comply with God's commands, becoming holy, as a consequence, the "ground of assurance" that we shall be brought into "everlasting felicity."[191]

Applying the wages of compliance in pursuit of happiness, Owen rejects any suggestion that the cost of compliance to God's law is a form of bondage. Yet compliance does not mean servility and is not inconsistent with the "free spirit of the children of God," and to say otherwise is a "vain imagination" to Owen, who

---

187. III:351.
188. III.613.
189. III:613.
190. III:613.
191. III.613.

believes that "a due respect unto God's promises and threatenings is a principal part of our liberty."¹⁹²

Laws Designed for the External Establishment of Religion Are Generally Ineffective

Owen regards a canon of civil law as an unsuitable basis for religion:¹⁹³ "It is true, that when the doctrine of religion is determined and established by civil laws" conformity to that religion issues "from that external cause alone."¹⁹⁴ He regards nations that impose some form of nominal Christianity, particularly in the form of liturgies, as endorsing in the popular mind "their peculiar errors."¹⁹⁵

The Entire Human Race Is Under the Condemnation of the Law of God

Owen bears witness to the condemnation of even the least transgression of the law. Under the old covenant, each command requires universal holiness. The very least failure, whether "in substance, circumstance, or degree," means that we have transgressed the law entire: "whosoever shall keep the whole law, and yet offend in one point, he is guilty of all" (James 2:10). (We cannot comply with the covenant of works because of our "lapsed condition.")¹⁹⁶

Not only is compliance impossible because of the covenant's universal requirements but because "no man influenced only by the commands of the law, or first covenant, absolutely considered, whatever in particular he might be forced or compelled unto, did ever sincerely aim or endeavour after universal holiness."¹⁹⁷ Not

192. III.613.
193. IV:243.
194. IV:243.
195. IV:243.
196. III:606.
197. III.606.

only is compliance impossible because men cannot do so, but because they will not.

Incomplete conformity and even the external appearance of holiness is possible, however. The law subdues some, who may be compelled to "habituate themselves unto a strict course of duty." Even incomplete obedience may sedate the conscience to some degree; just as impure motives may result in partial obedience, and a desire of applause, self-righteousness, or superstition may result in an appearance of holiness.[198]

Owen condemns the folly of the belief that holiness is derived solely in response to the commands of law, warning that this belief involves "tormenting disquietments" and deception.[199] Neither can salvation be procured merely by adhering to the letter of the law:

> And for this reason we are necessitated to deny a possibility of salvation unto all to whom the gospel is not preached, as well as unto those by who it is refused; for they are left unto this law, whose precepts they cannot answer, and whose end they cannot attain.[200]

Owen draws a distinction between those who keep the law under the covenant of works and those who keep it under the covenant of grace. Under either covenant the faithful are bound by some body of precepts, but those obeying the covenant of works do so that they might be justified in the sight of God. On the other hand, those who obey the covenant of grace do so lest their disobedience reflect dishonour upon the righteousness and holiness of the Gospel.[201]

---

198. III:606.
199. III:607
200. III:607.
201. III:608.

The Relation of the Law of God and the Regenerate

The Relation of the Law of God to the Life Calling of the Regenerate

Although a professional calling may be lawful, and those in that calling attend to it with industry and diligence, Owen remarks that our spiritual calling is more important, and should occupy us more[202]:

> It may be, it will be asked, whether it be necessary that men should think as much and as often about things spiritual and heavenly as they do about the lawful affairs of their callings? I say, more, and more often, if we are what we profess ourselves to be.

The Relation of the Law of God to the Sanctification of the Regenerate

All acts of a believer must be lawful:

> [It is] wrought and preserved in the minds and souls of all believers, by the Spirit of God, a supernatural principle or habit of grace and holiness, whereby they are made meet and enabled to live unto God, and perform that obedience which he requireth and accepteth through Christ in the covenant of grace; essentially or specifically distinct from all natural habits, intellectual and moral, however or by what means soever acquired or improved.[203]

God requires obedience to the law because it is the only means whereby we may express our subjection, our dependence on him, our fruitfulness and thankfulness; the only way of our communion and intercourse with him, of using and improving the effects of his love, the benefits of the mediation of Christ, whereby we may glorify him in this world; and the only orderly way whereby we

---

202. VII:302.
203. VII:302.

may be made meet for the inheritance of the saints in light: which is sufficient, in general, to manifest both its necessity and its use.[204]

The Law Is Given As a Rule of Obedience

Owen's view is that Paul valued the law because the "law was given of God immediately, as the whole and only rule of our obedience unto him." Paul considered the "nature, use, and end of the law," concluding that it is an insufficient means of our justification before God (Galatians 3:19-20).[205]

How the Believer Is To Fulfill the Law

Owen sees all separation from God as a curse that is connected to the law.[206] On our behalf Christ underwent such separation from God as the curse the law requires, and believers are united with God.[207] The power that separates God from believers is absorbed by Christ, who bore the full brunt.[208] Owen extols law's holiness: "There is in the whole law and every parcel of it an eternal, indispensable righteousness and truth, arising either from the nature of the things themselves concerning which it is, or the relation of one thing unto another."[209]

He sees the eternal verity, and righteousness of the law, both as a totality and the sum of its parts,[210] explaining that is no respecter of persons:

> The law doth not threaten a curse only if we do not believe, but if we do not all things written therein, Deuteronomy 27:26. Whether we believe or not, the law takes

---

204. III:472.
205. V:26.
206. XI:295.
207. XI:295.
208. XI:295.
209. XI:295.
210. XI:295.

no notice; as to the curse that is denounceth, if there hath been any sin, that must be execute. And the law is for the curse, as Isaac for the great spiritual blessing, Genesis 27:27-29.[211]

Owen argues that the "one great curse" was "undergone by Christ."[212]

Some Things, Although Lawful, May Become Dangerous If They Cause Others To Stumble

With abiding validity, the law prescribes what is lawful and what is unlawful in the worship of God. Some of what is lawful, however, may be a danger if it causes others to stumble.[213] For this reason, love disallows some of what is lawful in order to preserve and edify the sanctity of others.

Lawfulness of Forms of Prayer

Owen believes that "to compose and write forms of prayer for direction and doctrinal helps unto others, as to the matter and method to be used in the right discharge of this duty, is lawful, and may in some cases be useful." Forms of prayer may serve to divert the mind from the act of prayer itself, but nonetheless the forms instruct believers.[214]

CONCLUSION

Owen's breadth and depth of understanding is profound, demonstrated by his delineation of arguments, and explains that the law exposes sin but cannot save believers from its effects. Moreover, for Owen ceremonial law of the Old Testament is never abolished

211. XI:295.
212. XI:295.
213. XIII:347.
214. IV:347.

but transformed. (This applies only to the ceremonial corpus of the law.) Although he never explicitly says that nations are obligated to obey the Decalogue, in both case laws that interpret the Decalogue (*cf.* Exodus 21–23) and the sanctions enforcing the case laws (*cf.* Exodus 21–23), Owen's paradigm was theonomic, in the post-Rushdoony sense (Congregationalist Puritan colleagues who settled Massachusetts Bay certainly were). It is, however, awkward and problematic to apply modern categories to an era when no debate on theonomy existed. Nevertheless, Owen represents a freshening of the obligations of belief, as such a beacon for those today who would better understand the law and its place in the word of God.

THOMAS BOSTON'S VIEW OF SUBSTANTIVE BIBLICAL LAW

The Puritan Thomas Boston demonstrates a keen understanding of biblical law, his treatment of the covenant of works among the most extensive that Reformed literature offers, since he connects the first covenant, the covenant of works, and biblical law. Additionally, by his allegory of the conversation between a Gospel minister, an antinomian, a legalist, and a young Christian, he illustrates from life differences between these points of view.

THE PROPERTIES OF BIBLICAL LAW

Boston describes biblical law as universal, perfect, indispensable and perpetual, believing in the universality ascribed by Romans 2:14-15: "all men, in all places . . . and at all times."[1] Since Old Testament law lacks nothing, Christ did not have to add anything; it was already whole. Boston interprets Psalm 19:7 to mean that the New Testament itself adds nothing to the Old in this respect.[2] He sees the law as indispensable and perpetual, according to Luke 16:17, "every jot and tittle of the law," and Matthew 5:18, "one jot or one tittle shall in no wise pass from the law, till all be fulfilled."[3]

---

1. Thomas Boston, *The Works of the Late Rev. Thomas Boston* (Wheaton, Ill.: R. O. Roberts, 1980), II:62.
2. II:62.
3. II:62.

THE PURPOSE OF BIBLICAL LAW

Boston makes a distinction between the purpose of God's law before the fall and after. Originally, the law was revealed to Adam in his original state so that by obeying he would justify his existence. The purpose of the law since the fall of Adam is, however, threefold. First, the law's purpose is to tell everyone what the holy will of God is and what their duty is toward him (Micah 6:8).[4] The second purpose is to show people that they are unable to keep the law, thereby humbling them with the sense of their sin. Boston cites Psalm 19:11–12, "By them is thy servant warned. Who can understand his errors? Cleanse thou me from secret faults."[5]

The third purpose is to communicate a clear sense of our need of Christ. Galatians 3:19 states "Wherefore serveth the law? It was added because of transgressions, till the seed should come, to whom the promise was made." Boston explains the awakening of our need in three ways. The law convicts individuals of their sin, exposes God's wrath due to them, and awakens their consciences through actuating guilt (apprehension of misery, bondage, and fear, all of which reveal our need of Christ, and the perfection of his obedience).[6]

Boston also considers the law from the viewpoint of the unregenerate. For them, the law is a "looking-glass to let them see their state and case,"[7] as well as a "bridle to hold them with its commands and threatenings, who otherwise would regard nothing."[8] Boston sees the law as a "scourge, vexing and tormenting their consciences, and making them uneasy in a single course, rendering them inexcusable, and laying them under the curse."[9] He believes, therefore, that the law is an active force that impels the sinner with guilt.

4. II:63.
5. II:63.
6. II:63.
7. II:63.
8. II:63.
9. II:63.

Boston also considers the law from the perspective of those who are in Christ, for whom the law functions to magnify Christ: "shewing them their obligation to him for fulfilling it in their stead."[10] The law functions as a rule of life for believers, wherein they express their gratitude by obeying the law of Christ.[11]

In sum, Boston sees the law leading the unregenerate to Christ as Savior, who redeems them from its curse and condemnation, leading them to the law as a "directory, the rule and standard of their obedience."[12]

THE PENALTY FOR DISOBEDIENCE TO BIBLICAL LAW

Biblical Law and the Covenant of Works

God originally established a covenant of works for Adam that included both an element of grace and an element of law. The element of grace was God's provision of eternal life, and a companion, a garden, dominion over the earth, over plants, and animals, as well as communion with God. The legal element included both a negative and positive component with God's law written upon Adam's heart. The negative component was the prohibition to eat of the tree of life, the positive the command to keep the garden, to multiply, and to subdue the earth; the moral law written, as upon Adam's heart, was later codified, summarily, as the Ten Commandments.

The Penalty for Breach of the Covenant of Works

Boston believes that breaking of the covenant of works meant a twofold penalty, of both legal and real dimensions. The legal dimension of the penalty is death, ensuing from an "actual liableness

---

10. II:64.
11. II:64.
12. II:64.

to all miseries for satisfying offended justice"[13]: "cursed is every one that continueth not in all things which are written in the book of the law to do them" (Galatians 3:10).

> Thus was man to die the day he should break the covenant; and thus he died that very moment he sinned, because by his sin he broke the holy, just, and good law of God; set himself in opposition to his Creator.[14]

Boston illustrates legal death (Galatians 3:10):

> Thus the clouds gathered over his head, to shower down upon him; and thus was he girded with the cords of death, which neither himself nor any other creature could loose.[15]

The penalty for breaking the covenant of works is "real death," which includes spiritual death, natural death, and eternal death. Real death is the result of a sentence (Deuteronomy 29:19–20), for threatened evils and punishments are contained in the curse of the law.[16] Spiritual death is that of the soul and spirit, as described in Ephesians 2:1, the moral death of the soul by which it is "divested of the image of God, that is, saving knowledge, righteousness, and holiness."[17] In the state of spiritual death, sin preys upon the soul throughout the course of natural life:

> Sin laid the soul as it were in the grave, the house of death; and there being dead while the man liveth, devouring death works and preys in, and upon it, two ways—In the progress of sin and corruption in the soul, as the body in the grave rots more and more, Psalm 14:3. The soul being spiritually dead, the longer it lies in that case, them or loathsome and abominable it becomes. Swarms of reigning lusts breed in it, and are active therein; the remains of the image of God are defaced more and more in it, and

---

13. XI:207.
14. XI:207–8.
15. XI:208.
16. XI:208.
17. XI:208.

the soul still set farther off from God. All actual sins are the workings of this death, the motions of the verminating life of the soul in the grace of sin, Ephesians 2:1, 2. So that they are not only sins in themselves, but punishments of the first sin, which cannot cease to follow on God's departing from the soul; which may persuade us of the absurdity of that principle, that there is no sin in hell.[18]

In Boston's view, "sin preys upon the soul of man"

> the strokes of wrath on the soul. Where the carcass is, there these, like so many eagles, gather together. The sinning soul becomes the centre, wherein all manner of spiritual plagues meet together, as worms do in bodies interred, to feed thereon, Job 20:26. These are manifold; some of them felt, as sorrows, terrors, anxieties, losses, and troubles, crossing the man's will, and so vexing fretting, and disquieting him. Those are indeed a death to the soul, having a curse in them, like so many envenomed arrows shot into man; some of them not felt, so as to make the man groan under them, as blindness of mind, hardness of heart, strong delusions, but they are the more dangerous, as wounds that bleed inwardly.[19]

Not only does real death include spiritual death, but also natural death, which is death of the body, resulting from the separation of soul and body. This separation is of two kinds: stung and unstung death. Unstung death parts the soul and the body, but not by the curse of sin (1 Corinthians 15:55 says that death has no sting for the believer). Stung death is death by curse (Galatians 3:10).[20]

Real death also includes eternal death, which "issues from the eternal separation of both soul and body from God in hell" (Matthew 25:41),[21] bringing about a curse upon soul and body:

18. XI:209.
19. XI:210.
20. XI:211–12.
21. XI:213.

> This is the full accomplishment of the curse of the covenant of works; and presupposes the union of the soul and body, in a dreadful resurrection to damnation; the criminal soul and body being brought forth from their separate prisons and joined together again, that death may exercise its full force upon them for ever and ever.[22]

This separation of the united soul and body from God is "an irrecoverable loss of God's friendship, favour and image," Boston explains:

> No more communication for ever can be between God and the creature brought to this dreadful case. All passage of sanctifying influences is stopped; the curse lies on the creature, which bars all emanations of love and favour from heaven, and leaves it under unalterable barrenness. The holy frame of the soul marred by sin, must remain so, never to be mended.[23]

He interprets Mark 9:44 to mean that in hell, a united soul and body remain in "perpetual bitter despair,"[24] and furthermore are condemned to continual sinning:

> Think and act they must; and how can they but sin, when their corrupt nature remains with them in hell? Submission to just punishment is their duty; but how can they do that in whose hearts is not the least measure of God's grace? Nay, they will gnash their teeth, in rage against God.[25]

The reason for eternal death is that offenses against an infinite God are paid for by infinite suffering:

> Because they can not pay out the debt to the full, therefore must they ever lie in the prison. The wrong done by sin to the honour of God is an infinite one, because done against an infinite God; and therefore the satisfaction

22. XI:213.
23. XI:214.
24. XI:214.
25. XI:214.

can never be completed by the finite sufferer. So the yoke of punishment is wreathed about the neck of the sinner for ever and ever, never to be taken off.[26]

THREE CATEGORIES OF BIBLICAL LAW

For Boston, there are three kinds of law: ceremonial, judicial, and moral. The ceremonial law was given by Moses and "bound only the Jews" until the coming of Christ.[27] Boston holds that Christ "abrogated" this law because it was a "shadow of good things that were then to come: a hedge and partition-wall betwixt them and the Gentiles, which is now taken down."[28]

Judicial law was the civil law of the Jews, also given by Moses to regulate the "civil concerns" of the nation, "in respect of which the Jewish government was a Theocracy."[29] Boston's view of judicial law is significant; he states that although it made them a "happy people under such a government," it does "not bind other nations farther than it is of moral equity."[30] Moreover, judicial law should not bind other nations beyond "moral equity" because it was "peculiarly adapted to the circumstances of that nation."[31]

Moral law is "the declaration of the will of God to mankind, binding all men to perfect obedience thereto in all the duties of holiness and righteousness." On the other hand, ceremonial law was given to the Jews "as a church,"[32] just as the judicial law was given in their particular circumstances "as a state." The moral law, however, was given to the Jews "in common with all mankind."[33]

---

26. XI:214–15.
27. II:60.
28. II:60.
29. II:60.
30. II:61.
31. II:61.
32. II:61.
33. II:61.

THE MORAL LAW IN PARTICULAR

The Moral Law Before Sinai

Before the Decalogue was written by the finger of God at Sinai and recorded in the Torah through Moses, "all the race of Adam had a law written in their hearts."[34] Boston calls this law the "light of reason,"[35] further describing it as the "dictates of natural conscience."[36] These were moral principles that show good and evil to have an "essential equity" and are the "measures of his duty to God, to himself, and to his fellow-creatures."[37]

Boston defines the law written in the heart such as did Paul in Romans 12:2. The original law, says Boston, was "holy, just, and good," defining "holy" as "conformity to those attributes and actions of God, which are the pattern of our imitation." "Just" is "exactly agreeable to the frame of man's faculties, and most suitable to his condition in the world," while "good" means "beneficial to the observer of it, for 'in keeping of it there is great reward.' "[38]

In his state of innocence, Adam was an unadulterated image of God, comprised of the moral qualities and perfections of the soul, for the Lord had imparted to Adam "a spark of his own comeliness, in order to communicate with himself in happiness. This was an universal and entire rectitude in his faculties, disposing them to their proper operations."[39]

In the fallen state, Adam retained vestiges of the moral law. Common notions of good and evil, including that there is a God, that He is to be worshipped, and that we should give every one his due are what remains to us of the moral law written originally upon the heart.[40] Laws that are "common in all countries for the

---

34. II:60.
35. II:60.
36. II:60.
37. II:60.
38. II:60.
39. II:60.
40. II:61.

preserving of human societies" issue from these vestiges. "What standard else can they have for these laws but common reason?" The purpose of such laws, common to all countries, is societal preservation, the encouragement of virtue, and discouragement of vice.[41] Boston also sees an economic purpose: "The design of them is to keep men within the bounds of goodness for mutual commerce."[42] As progeny of Adam, we retain inward evidence of the remaining vestiges of the moral law. "Every man," according to Boston, "finds law within him that checks him if he offends it." "None are without a legal indictment, and a legal executioner, within them."[43]

The Relation of the Original Natural Law and the Covenant of Works

Boston sees the original natural law as beginning from the time of Adam's creation, before they were incorporated into the covenant of works in the Garden of Eden.[44] As Boston explains: "The natural law was in being when there was no covenant of works; for the former was given to man in his creation, without paradise; the latter was made with him after he was brought into paradise" (Genesis 2:7–8, 15–17).[45] The "chief matter" of the covenant of works was the original natural law[46]: "It was a rule of life to Adam before the covenant of works, and it may, yea and must be a rule of life to believers, after the covenant of works, and in that covenant a rule of life to Adam and all his natural seed."[47]

---

41. II:61.
42. II:61.
43. II:61.
44. XI:191.
45. XI:191–92.
46. XI:191.
47. XI:192.

Boston distinguishes natural law from the covenant of works. In the first place, original natural law did not promise of eternal life[48]; in the second, it did not threaten sinners with death.[49] Boston speculates that after the Creation (Genesis 1) and the institution of the covenant of works (Genesis 2), God could have "annihilated his creature" because He had not bound himself to give eternal life.[50] Since original natural law was built into Adam's psyche, "why may it not be made the matter of the law of Christ, and therein be a rule of life to them that are his?"[51]

In an aside, Boston pleads with the reader to "see their deep concern in this covenant; and consider that your help is not therein, but in laying hold on Christ, the head of the second covenant."[52] Original natural law and the covenant of works are "several links in one chain, constitutions of the Supreme Lawgiver, which, in point of obedience, stood and fell together."[53]

Boston discerns yet another law, to which Adam yielded obedience. Boston calls this third law "the positive symbolical law." God did not forbid Adam to eat of the tree of knowledge because of any evil in the tree. "It was not forbidden because it was evil; but evil because forbidden." Although this point may be only "minute," Boston notes that it is in the "most minute things God appears greatest."[54]

Boston believes that God established a symbolical law with the purpose of making a point regarding his will. The symbolical law was a test of Adam, whose obedience to this law would be the "most glaring evidence of true obedience," while he was in his pristine state.[55] Whether be believed in another god, created no graven images, did not blaspheme or keep the Sabbath were inappropriate

48. XI:192.
49. XI:192.
50. XI:192.
51. XI:192.
52. XI:192.
53. XI:192.
54. XI:193.
55. XI:193.

laws for him while ever he lived in a pristine state.[56] Furthermore, these laws were not an adequate demonstration of obedience until Eve came from his own flesh.[57]

Symbolical law was appropriate to Adam's pristine state for other reasons: in the first place, Adam shared the nature of God; in the second, Adam had a pure nature, at least originally[58]: "Thus his obedience or disobedience behooved to be most clear, conspicuous, and undeniable; forasmuch as this law respected an external thing obvious to sense, and the discerning of any, who yet could not judge internal acts of obedience or disobedience. So that God might be 'clear in judging,' Psalm 51:4, in the eyes of angels good and bad, and of man himself."[59] To Boston, the tree was a "visible badge" of obedience, as he explains, "It was most proper for asserting God's dominion over man, being a visible badge of man's subjection to God. God had made him lord of the inferior world, set him down in paradise, a place furnished with all things for necessity and delight; so it was becoming the divine wisdom and sovereign dominion, to discharge him from meddling with one tree in the garden, as a testimony of his holding all of him as his great Landlord."[60]

Boston calls one who seeks eternal life by means of keeping the law a "self-justiciary."[61] In order to avoid this destiny, we are obliged to keep to the severity of the law; as Christ states in Matthew: "If thou wilt enter into life keep the commandments" (Matthew 19:17). Boston understands "the commandments" as the Ten Commandments, seeing them as the summation of the "whole moral law."[62]

The origin of the Ten Commandments is twofold: the audible voice of God and the finger of God:

56. XI:193.
57. XI:193.
58. XI:193.
59. XI:193.
60. XI:193.
61. II:66.
62. II:66.

> Never was law given in such a solemn manner, with such dread and awful majesty, Exodus 19; Deuteronomy 4:5; Hebrews 12:18. The people were commanded to wash their clothes before the law was delivered them. By this, as in a type, the Lord required the sanctifying of their ears and hearts to receive it. There were bounds and limits set to the mount, that it might breed in the people dread and reverence to the law, and to God the holy and righteous Lawgiver. There were great thunderings and lightnings. The artillery of heaven was shot off at that solemnity, and therefore it is called 'a fiery law.' The angels attended at the delivery of the law. The heavenly militia, to speak so, were all mustered out on this important occasion. In a word, the law was promulgated with marks of supreme majesty; God by all this shewing how a vain thing it is for sinners to expect life by the works of the law; and thereby also shewing the necessity of a Mediator.[63]

God's purpose in choosing to deliver the law in a certain way was to humble believers. If they see their own insignificance before the majesty of the divine holiness, then they will also understand that they cannot achieve life eternal by means of the law.[64] God delivered the law from his own hand, for Moses received "immediately from God himself" two tables of stone (Exodus 31). God used stone for two reasons, says Boston: that he might "hold out the perpetuity of the law" and secondly, that he might show "withal the hardness of men's hearts."[65] Moses cast down the tablets, in Boston's view, because he was preserving their integrity by preventing the rebellious people from making sport of the tablets.[66]

The second tables were hewn by Moses and engraved by the finger of God, an event Boston interprets to mean: The sinner is "hewn" by the law, that is, the law defines the sinner to be what he is. As the sinner is saved, God gives the sinner a new fleshy heart whereupon "the spirit of Gospel-grace is the law written upon the

---

63. II:66–67.
64. II:67.
65. II:67.
66. II:67.

heart."⁶⁷ Boston believes this was the world's first alphabetic writing and that Moses derived the alphabet directly from God.⁶⁸ To Boston, alphabetic written language began with a divine miracle.⁶⁹

The Reason the Moral Law Was Given

The moral law was given because our inner nature is defective and cannot lead us to God; it is defective for several reasons,⁷⁰ in the first place, because it cannot expose the original cause of man's misery, Adam's first sin⁷¹: "Mere natural light can never teach a man to feel the weight and curse of sin committed some thousands of years before he was born, or to mourn for that filthiness, which he contracted in his conception, and for those sproutings of sin in his nature."⁷²

Secondly, natural judgment is "thoroughly distorted and infatuated, so that it is ready to reckon evil good, and good evil, light darkness and darkness light."⁷³ Thirdly, the inner law of nature is defective because it does not "drive men out of themselves for a remedy." Boston concludes:

> The sublimest philosophy that ever was did never teach a man to deny himself, but always taught him to build up his house with the old ruins, and to fetch stores and materials out of the wonted quarry. Shame, humiliation, confusion of face, self-abhorrence, condemning ourselves, and flying to the righteousness of another, are virtues known only in the book of God, and which the learned philosophers would have esteemed both irrational and pusillanimous things.⁷⁴

67. II:67.
68. II:67.
69. II:67.
70. II:67–68.
71. II:67.
72. II:67–68.
73. II:68.
74. II:68.

Lastly, the inner law is defective because in nature "men never knew nor had experience of a better state, and therefore must needs be ignorant of that full image of God in which it was created." Boston illustrates the limitations of natural man:

> As a man born and brought up in a dungeon is unable to conceive the state of the palace; or as the child of a nobleman stolen away, and brought up by some beggar, cannot conceive or suspect the honours of his blood; so corrupted nature is utterly unable, that has been born in a womb of ignorance, bred in a hell of uncleanness, and enthralled from the beginning to the prince of darkness, to conceive, or convince a man of, that most holy and pure condition in which he was created.[75]

The moral law was given to prevent our knowledge of God's revelation from perishing.

Perfect Law-Keeping Necessary To Escape the Wrath of God

Boston explains that to escape the wrath of God, one must keep the law perfectly,[76] and since none can do so, the lawbreaker must be united with Christ, the lawkeeper. (Christ perfectly kept the covenant of works.)[77] "Whosoever then would enter into the covenant of grace, must, in the first place, have a faith of the law; which therefore is necessary to be preached to sinners."[78] Because of faith in the law, the sinner, a "breaker of the law's commands, liable to divine vengeance," finds the need for grace.[79] As Boston elaborates:

> By the law man believes, that he is a lost and undone sinner, under the curse of the law for his sin, Galatians 3:10. He no more looks on the curse of the law as some strange

---

75. II:68.
76. II:395.
77. VII:215.
78. I:360.
79. I:360.

thing, belonging only to some monsters of wickedness, and far from him. But the Spirit of God brings home the dreadful sentence of that broken law, and applies it close to him, as if he had said, 'thou art the man.' And he groans out his belief thereof under the felt weight thereof, like a man under the sentence of death, Romans 7:9.[80]

The Law As the Rule of Life for Believers

Boston explains law as a rule for life by means of an allegory. Four parties, each representing an aspect of law, engage in conversation. "Evangelista," or the Gospel minister, represents a biblical view; "Neophitus," or the young Christian, asks about the place of law in the life of a believer; "Nomista," or the legalist, speaks for the legalistic view of sanctification (a believer is sanctified by means of law-works); "Antinomista," or antinomian, represents the view that law has no part in a believer's sanctification. Like Bunyan, Boston personified doctrines to great effect pedagogicially.[81]

Boston entertains the views of Luther in his commentary on Galatians and of Calvin in his *Institutes*: "The conscience hath nothing to do with the law or works" (Luther),[82] and he draws on Calvin: "The conscience of the faithful, when the affiance of their justification before God is to be sought, must raise and advance themselves above the law, and forget the whole righteousness of the law, and lay aside all thinking upon works."[83] Boston uses "Evangelista" to explain Luther and Calvin; neither referred to the law in these quotes except in reference to justification.[84] Justification is not by works, but according to Boston, when a believer obeys the law in sanctification through the power of the Holy Spirit, then he

---

80. I:360.
81. VII:305ff.
82. VII:312.
83. VII:313.
84. VII:313.

is also keeping the law of Christ. Thus manifest, the law of Christ neither justifies nor condemns.[85]

The Ten Commandments and Adam's Creation

Comparing Genesis 1:27 with Ephesians 4:24, Boston concludes that the law given to Adam, and Adam himself, were both "created righteous and holy.[86] Boston sees the "natural law" and the "law of the ten commandments" as one in essence.[87] "All things which are written in the book of the law" (Galatians 3:10) inform a single legal entity, whether viewed as natural law or as Scripture.[88] Boston believes that Adam knew the corpus of divine law.[89] To Boston, knowledge of the law is essential to righteousness[90]—he equates Adam's knowledge of the law and Adam's original righteousness with the image of God.[91] Among the heathen, Boston perceives the "remains" of the law originally imparted into Adam's being: "the same law which God gave from Sinai with thunder and lightning, in all the precepts of it was breathed into Adam's soul, when God breathed into him the breath of life and he became a living soul."[92] For Boston, "all created righteousness and holiness" is "conformity to the moral law;"[93] the law of God is fundamental to Adam's creation (*cf.* Ecclesiastes 7:29).[94]

No sooner did Adam exist than he embodied the law of God.[95] "He was no sooner a man than he was a righteous man, knowing the natural law he was under, and being conformed to it in the

85. VII:313.
86. XI:191.
87. XI:191
88. XI:191.
89. XI:191.
90. XI:191.
91. XI:191.
92. XI:191.
93. XI:191.
94. XI:191.
95. XI:191.

powers and faculties of his soul."⁹⁶ Boston defines natural law as the law surrounding Adam at the Creation.⁹⁷ Matthew 22:37–39 is the sum of natural law or the law of the Ten Commandments: the first and greatest is "Thou shalt love the Lord thy God with all thy heart, and with all they soul, and with all thy mind" and the second, "Thou shalt love thy neighbor as thyself."⁹⁸

THE DIFFERENCE BETWEEN BIBLICAL LAW AND THE GOSPEL

Biblical Law Is Partially Inherent; the Gospel Is Not

Boston describes the law as a part of our natures after the fall. The law is a doctrine that teaches us there is a God, and what God is, and what he requires us to do, "binding all reasonable creatures to perfect obedience, both internal and external, promising the favour of God, and everlasting life to all those who yield perfect obedience thereunto, and denouncing the curse of God and everlasting damnation to all those who are not perfectly correspondent thereunto."⁹⁹

The Gospel, however, is not inherently known and understood, but rather "is a doctrine revealed from heaven by the Son of God."¹⁰⁰

The Preaching of the Law Is Necessary, But Only the Gospel Saves

According to Boston, preaching the law is necessary because it teaches sinners of their need for Christ:

---

96. XI:191.
97. XI.191.
98. XI:191.
99. VIII:459.
100. VIII:459.

> He that would engraft, must needs use the pruning-knife. Sinners have many contrivances to keep them from Christ; many things by which they keep their hold of the natural stock; there they have need to be closely pursued, and hunted out of their skulking holes, and refuges of lies.[101]

Boston interprets the "law" in Romans 6:14 to mean the covenant of works; believers are not under that covenant either to be justified or condemned thereby.[102] Because Christ gave perfect obedience to the covenant of works, the believer is not condemned by the law, for Christ's obedience satisfied the law's demands, and it can demand nothing of believers.[103] Christ's passive obedience also satisfied the law because He suffered its punishment ("having suffered the very penalty threatened therein").[104] In following Christ, therefore, believers have no law against them, because in Christ they agree with the law in letter and in spirit.[105]

BIBLICAL LAW AND THE DISTINCTION OF CHURCH AND STATE

Boston distinguishes between the law of the state and that pertaining to government of Christ's kingdom[106]:

> The kings of the earth have no ground to grudge the kingdom of Christ its freedom in their dominions; seeing it is a spiritual kingdom, and quite of another nature than the kingdoms of this world; and interferes not with any of the just rights and prerogatives of earthly crowns. Yet how sad is it that this kingdom should be an eye-sore

---

101. VIII:200.
102. II:64.
103. II:64.
104. II:64.
105. II:64.
106. I:486.

to the kings of the earth, and that they should employ their power to suppress and bear it down?[107]

He endorses the concept of sphere sovereignty—the distinction of church and state. Although one may influence the other, both must operate in separate spheres.

Boston highlights the duty of magistrates toward their public. First, they must establish good laws, and see them duly executed (Zechariah 14:9 and 2 Chronicles 19:5–7). Second, they must govern with wisdom, justice, and clemency (2 Chronicles 1:10). Third, they must punish evildoers, and encourage them that do well according to Romans 13:3.[108] Fourth, they must protect citizens, and provide for their common safety (1 Timothy 2:2), as well as see to their prosperity, and not oppress them (Proverbs 28:16).[109] Fifth, magistrates "ought to promote true religion, and advance the interest of Christ's kingdom among their subjects" (Isaiah 49:23 in support: "and kings shall be thy nursing fathers, and their queens thy nursing mothers: they shall bow down to thee with their face toward the earth, and lick up the dust of thy feet; and thou shalt know that I am the Lord: for they shall not be ashamed that wait for me").[110]

Boston rebuts Knox, who argues that believers have not only the right but the responsibility to overthrow wicked rulers:

> Let us be dutiful to subordinate magistrates under him, and honour those whom God has honoured by their office, saying to them, 'ye are gods.' Let us not stumble as theists, Jacobites, and malignants, against our holy religion, by contempt of the magistrate. We read the Bible, where subjection is commanded to subjects oft and again, even to magistrates that were enemies to Christianity. We are the followers of that Jesus who paid his tribute, and taught the people of the Jews, who were more solemnly covenanted with God, and more strictly bound up in the

---

107. I:486.
108. II:249.
109. II:250.
110. II:250.

choice of their kings, than any nation under heaven, yet not to deny their tribute to Caesar, the Heathen Roman emperor, who then was their chief magistrate.

In addition, Boston draws on Matthew 22:19–21 to support his ideas on government (Jesus paid taxes with Peter to the Roman government.)[111]

CONCLUSION

The works of Thomas Boston reflect a keen understanding of the function of biblical law as a focus for other branches of theology. In the current theological debate, Boston is not a "theonomist," because he believed that the judicial law of Israel was peculiar to Israel—Mosaic judicial sanctions are inappropriate to other nations. Judicial law, "peculiarly adapted to the circumstances of that nation," Israel, should not bind other nations beyond "moral equity."[112] Boston does not define what he means by "moral equity," leaving us with food for thought, since it occupies a central position in his arguments. "Moral equity," like "general equity" of the Westminster Confession, inspires passionate disagreements.

THOMAS GOODWIN'S VIEW OF SUBSTANTIVE BIBLICAL LAW

Thomas Goodwin's dying words are indicative: "I think I cannot love Christ better than I do. I am swallowed up in God"; Goodwin's life reflects the Spirit of God. During the Puritan era, Goodwin was converted at the University of Cambridge, a hotbed of Congregationalist Puritanism. Later, from 1625–34, he served as a Fellow and Lecturer at St. Catherine's Hall, Cambridge. His teaching and preaching ministry took him to Magdalen College, Oxford, where as President, he and John Owen were colleagues. Perhaps this team of powerful preachers, in time marked by revival, as well

---

111. II:250.
112. II:61.

as doctrinal, social, and political reforms, is without parallel in post-Apostolic Church history.[113]

Goodwin's overall doctrine of the law of God is articulated in the 19th chapter of the Westminster Confession of Faith of 1648, and the parameters explicated in questions 91–150 of the Larger Catechism. The seven theses of the Westminster Confession on the law of God outline the breadth and depth of Goodwin's thought.[114] According to Nichol's *Complete Works of Thomas Goodwin*, Goodwin's exposition of the doctrine of the law of God may be categorized around three foci—the nature of the law of God, the function of the law of God, and the relationship between Christ and the law of God.

THE NATURE OF THE LAW OF GOD

Definition and Origin

What is the law? Goodwin defines the law as the "will, word, and command of the great God."[115] Goodwin sees Christ himself as the embodiment of the law, but, "in a higher and more glorious sense," the law is actually a copy of Christ, who is the original. The law is a copy of "what is substantial in him." As the full expression of the Father and the paradigm of the natural and written law of God, Christ is called "ὁ λόγος" the Divine Word (*cf.* John 1:1). Moreover, not only is Christ the paradigm but also the founder and giver of the law (*cf.* Galatians 3:19), so that both the natural and written law originate from Christ himself. In the Scriptures, Christ as the originator of the law became its "servant" and "apprentice." Christ was made "under the law" (Galatians 4:4), and willingly entered a bond with the law, gave the law power over him, and made himself

113. Thomas Goodwin, *The Work of the Holy Spirit in Our Salvation* (Carlisle: The Banner of Truth Trust, 1979), jacket introduction.

114. The Confession of Faith. The Larger and Shorter Catechisms, with the Scripture Proofs at Large: Together with the Sum of Saving Knowledge. (Glasgow: Free Presbyterian Publications, 1985), pp. 79–84, 91–150.

115. Thomas Goodwin, *The Works of Thomas Goodwin* (Edinburgh: James Nichol, 1861–1863), V:131.

a debtor to the law in order to fulfill it.[116] The law of God illumines Christ its author as Christ illumines the law of God; and so Christ fulfilled the law that He himself gave.

Purposes

According to Goodwin, the law of God has two purposes: the negative, to reveal sin and God's attitude toward it, and the positive, to guide mankind to please God. He identifies clearly the aim of God's law: "Now the ends and grounds of giving God's law were to declare and shew forth his justice and hatred against sin wherever he found it."[117] The law is God's revelation of his thoughts and feelings toward sin.[118]

Not only does Goodwin hold to a negative purpose of the law (revealing sin), he sees a positive purpose (guiding mankind). Goodwin describes law as a guiding knowledge in three ways: first, by citing the Greek philosophical term "ἡγεομαι," or knowledge that "guides men in all their ways," implying that knowledge guides actions, or that ideas have practical consequences. To the pagan, philosophy was the system of values, beliefs, and ethics that guided his every action. To the Christian, the law is God's articulation of an impeccable system of values, beliefs, and ethics to govern his every action. Second, Goodwin uses metonymy to describe the law (Romans 7:3). The points of analogy between this metonymy and its referent, the law, are threefold. As a husband is near to the wife, so the law is to be near the heart of the Christian (*cf.* Psalm 40:8). As the husband guides the wife of his youth, so the law guides the Christian. As the husband protects and edifies his wife, so the law protects and nourishes law-abiding Christians.[119]

---

116. V:131.
117. V:490.
118. V:18.
119. IV:167.

Components

Literal and Spiritual Aspects

To Goodwin, there is a literal as well as spiritual dimension of the law; the dimensions are not contradictory because there is but one law, the difference being in the nature of the lawkeeper. Paul observed this difference in Romans 7:6, "but now we are delivered from the law, that being dead wherein we were held; that we should serve in newness of spirit, and not in the oldness of the letter." The oldness of the letter, according to Goodwin, is the "frame of heart accompanying it in the old man, or in a man's unregenerate estate." This "oldness" is explained in 2 Corinthians 5:17, where it refers to the entire unregenerate state—"old things are passed away, behold all things are become new." Christians should, therefore, serve in "newness of the spirit," that is, in a renewed and spiritual frame of heart.[120] To Goodwin, the spirit of the law does not deny the latter but includes it. Of course, the unregenerate may perceive only the letter—the bare outward essentials; on the other hand, the new man may perceive the spirit of the law—the outward essentials plus the inward disposition to obey out of love of the Lawgiver. Obedience must include the spirit as well as outward conformity with the letter of the law. "As the body without the soul is dead, so would these commandments or duties, performed thus only according to the letter but be the dead letter of the law; for the spirit that should inspire them with that which is their proper life, would be still wanting."[121]

Preceptive and Penal Elements

According to Goodwin, the law of God, like any other law, has "two main parts," preceptive and penal. The preceptive part is apprehended by the imperative "do this and live," and this "requires

---

120. VI:262.
121. VI:263.

exact obedience to every tittle of it."[122] The penal part is apprehended: "if we trespass in the least, it exacts a punishment; and this is eternal death."[123] The nature of the debt incurred for trespass to sin is a "double debt." The laws of men often require twofold satisfaction—restitution to the party wronged and a further punishment or fine as a "satisfaction to the law itself."

> For in such trespasses there is a double wrong: the one to the party injured, whose goods or honour is impaired; and the other to the law, which is scandalized by it. And so he is not only to satisfy for the personal damage, but also for the public offense, and the vitiosity of the act in breaking order; and so a double satisfaction is to be made.[124]

Goodwin then illustrates the same principle in the economic and ceremonial realms:

> Thus also it is in debts: for there is both the principal, and the forfeiture also. So likewise in the Levitical law, when a man had wronged his neighbour in goods, he was to do two things; not only to make restitution due to the party wronged, and that double at least, as part of a punishment also, but he was to satisfy the law besides, and to offer sacrifice. And in case of debt, before instanced, until a man hath paid it, he is to lie in prison, to satisfy the law.[125]

Moral and Ceremonial Elements

Goodwin "long observed" that the moral and ceremonial categories of the law were "put together" according to Hebrews 9:15–19. The reason for this fusion, and its performance, suited the Jewish

---

122. V:85.
123. V:85.
124. V:85
125. V:85.

nation because they were a national church.[126] Goodwin affirms the Christian abrogation of Jewish ceremonial law: "I acknowledge it [the ceremonial law] given *de novo* to the Jews, though fallen, as they were a church; but this being proper to the Jews, hath no influence or relation to all the temporaries under the Gospel." He acknowledges its value to the unregenerate. Even though Paul was guided by Jewish law to a state of external righteousness (*cf.* Philippians 3), Goodwin holds that the same law was actually given as a covenant only to the elect among the Jews.[127] Further, Goodwin sees in Christ a "great and eminent change" from the legal economy of Moses. "With the change of the high priest, there must needs be a change of the law." Moses' ceremonial law is "said to speak on earth" (*cf.* Hebrews 9:25) but Christ is said to have brought new law that is heavenly in opposition to it (*cf.* Hebrews 9:23).[128]

Characteristics

Glorious

Goodwin calls the law glorious in two respects, its content[129] and initial administration.[130] The content of God's law is glorious because all that God made bears his image and "whatsoever holds forth the image of God hath a glory in it, for the least ray or beam of God hath glory in it." The law was made by God. Therefore, the law bears the glory of God.

Proceeding by syllogism and verbal parallelism, Goodwin claims God's law is glorious. In 1 Corinthians 11:7, this glory and God's image "are made all one."[131]

---

126. VI:355.

127. VI:356.

128. V:456. "It is true, the tenor and letter of the law is dispensed with, but not the debt; that is a fully exacted as ever." Goodwin believes that the debts incurred under Old Testament law could only be paid by Christ. V:490.

129. IV:315–16.

130. IV:315.

131. IV:316.

> The law, I told you, was a glorious law, because it continued the image of God, so far as dead letters could hold forth that image. The law written in Adam's heart was the image of God, and that being blotted out, God took a copy of what was in Adam's heart, so that indeed the law is rather an image of the image of God, than the image of God properly; it is but the image of the image that was in Adam's heart, and but a literal picture of it.[132]

To Goodwin, "All have sinned, and come short of the glory of God (Romans 3:23)" means that none have lived up to the image of God in natural man. "So I think it is the best interpretation, or at leastwise one great part of the meaning." Goodwin says that all mankind are "fallen from that grace and righteousness which at first God did implant in them, by which they were justified, and so are come short of the favour of God, which did shine upon them." And since the gospel is glorious in 2 Corinthians 4:4 because it holds forth Jesus Christ as the image of God, so the law, containing the image of God, "had a glory in it materially."[133]

Not only in its content, but also in its initial administration or promulgation, does Goodwin see the law as glorious. When God "came to give the law," he "attended with" glory. The initial administration of the law resembles the "day of judgment," so says Goodwin, drawing on Exodus 19:

> For God, when he came to give the law to sinners, came down from heaven and placed his tabernacle upon Mount Sinai, like unto a judge, attended with glorious angels (for 'the law was given by angels'), and with many glorious miracles, thunder, and earthquake, and fire, and smoke, and the sound of the trumpet.[134]

And so the earthly parallel:

> Even as the glory of a kingdom is most seen when they go to enact laws, for then the king and all the nobles go in their parliament robes; and so your judges, when they go

---

132. IV:317.
133. IV:316.
134. IV:316.

to execute the laws, to condemn men, go attended with the sound of a trumpet, and halberds, and etc.[135]

Such a divine visitation, with an entourage of angels, and so forth, adds luster to the glory of the Lawgiver.

Weak on Account of the Flesh

Goodwin's interpretation of the controversial "weak through the flesh" (Romans 8:3) is as follows: as we know from Deuteronomy, "he dealt not so with any nation, neither have the heathen the knowledge of this law," implying that God gave a common light of nature to all nations, in addition to which was the light of his law. Although Jews were subject to the same laws as Adam, the revelations of Mosaic law contributed more to their betterment. Goodwin asks, "How cometh it to pass that the law could do no good, could not work upon men's hearts, though a Spirit went with it? (*cf.* Neh. 9:20)." He answers from Romans 8:3, "What the law could not do, in that it was weak through the flesh"; "corrupt nature weakened all the power" of the law. Flesh perverted the pure meaning of the law so that its convicting power was limited, rendering it weak in effect, its potentiality non-functional. One who excelled in obedience to the moral law, such as Socrates, and one who excelled in outward conformity to Mosaic law, such as Paul, were outstanding, but unable to merit salvation by legal obedience. (Goodwin interprets the statement, "I have kept a good conscience to this day" as a testimony that Paul had never sinned against his conscience.) The law, therefore, was "weak" on account of the flesh.

THE FUNCTION OF THE LAW

Reflects Divine Honor

To Goodwin, the law of God is a reflection of God's honor, the law imprinted with his nature:

---

135. IV:316.

God's laws, especially his first command, is but the copy and extract of Gods' most holy, righteous, and blessed will, and many of his commands are the copy of his most holy nature, as that of this first command, as such which he in his nature is inclined to will and command; and therefore his law is called holy as he is holy, and being written in the heart doth renew us in his image.[136]

Hence, every breach of divine law is an act of treason.[137] Such treason is "against the Lord," and "provoke[s] the eyes of his glory" (Isaiah 3:8).[138] Goodwin believes that despising God's law is more heinous than despising any of God's deeds:

> To despise any of God's works, and slight them is a dishonour to the Maker, as Solomon says; but to slight his law is more, because that his transcendent excellency and kingly authority are thus engaged in it.[139]

And Goodwin asserts the reason:

> Kings indeed, in their laws, do not lay all the weight of their authority upon every law, but God doth. And therefore every sin is not only a transgression of his will, but a debasement of the sovereignty of his will. Hence in the promulgation of God's laws there runs this preface, 'I am the Lord thy God'; therefore do this, Exodus 20:1. So that his sovereignty is slighted in every sin, and in it there is a contempt of his crown and dignity.[140]

---

136. X:114.
137. X:114.
138. X:113.
139. V:94.
140. V:94.

Demands Human Holiness

Demands Holiness by Universal Testimony

Because it is universal and natural testimony emerging from the hearts of all men, the law communicates man's need of holiness, in support of which, Goodwin cites Romans 2:14–15:

> [The text] gives instance in the Gentiles, (whom all acknowledge under wroth and unregeneracy), and their having the effects of the law written by nature. And above all other effects of the law, he instanceth in conscience accusing and excusing, as that which of all other argues the law written there.[141]

To Paul, the law is ingrained in the hearts of Gentiles (Romans 2:14–15), to a degree so powerful and prevailing in many of them that the prints of them were published and stamped in fair characters in their lives; that is, they acted according to it. The "eminent principle or seat of this effect of the law" is the conscience, says Goodwin. The function of the conscience is to excuse and approve, and pronounce a sentence of absolution and justification, "both to their actions and persons, when they do well; as also when they do ill, it again at other times accuseth."[142] The moral law as written upon men's hearts sits as an inner judge upon actions and attitudes. Even all the stirrings of conscience of men in hell are good, "as they are from God and the Spirit of bondage."[143]

Goodwin contrasts the writing of the law upon one's heart with the writing of sin thereon (*cf.* Jeremiah 17:1). Both are character traits which nest in the inner man:

> We may fitly understand what it is to have Gods' law written in the heart, by what is meant by the writing its contrary, namely, sin and corruption, in the heart, Jeremiah 17:1. There sin is said to be written in their hearts, as with the point of a diamond, that is deeply engraven.

141. VI:234.
142. VI:234.
143. VI:262.

> Now what manner of letters these are wherewith sin is written on our hearts, we have woeful and daily experience of. They are letters suitable to the paper they are written on.[144]

Paul also explains that as sin is written upon the heart, so is righteousness written upon a regenerate heart. Goodwin cites 2 Corinthians 3:3 to illustrate, "Forasmuch as ye are manifestly declared to be the epistle of Christ ministered by us, written not with ink, but the Spirit of the living God; not in tables of stone, but in fleshy tables of the heart." This law, says the apostle, "is written, not with ink, but with the Spirit of the living God; not in tables of stone, but in the fleshly tables of the heart" (2 Corinthians 3).

Some object to being called to account over God's law in the heart because they are not written down, to which Goodwin replies: first, Christ himself writes this law into the hearts of all men, including the fallen:

> Our Redeemer's head was in the making of that law; and that the hand of him who was the 'Mighty Counselor,' did guide the pen that wrote it in Adam's heart at first; and further, that himself is the substantial image of God, and the "πρωτότυπον" of the law. And besides, when it was lost, and no copy on earth to be found, he it was that wrote it in the consciences of men fallen.[145]

He draws support for doctrine that Christ writes moral law on the heart from John 1:9, where the Divine Logos "enlightens every man that comes into the world." Next he deals with the claim that law written upon the heart is an imperfect copy, citing Psalm 19:7: "The law of the Lord is perfect, converting the soul: the testimony of the Lord is sure, making wise the simple." To clarify this law written upon the heart, the Lord renewed it upon Mt. Sinai according to Galatians 3:19. Further, Christ came in the fullness of time and "vindicated" the law "from all corrupt glosses in his preaching, fulfilled it in his life, and in fulfilling it, wrote it out

---

144. VI:403.
145. V:102.

again with his own hands, and so set a more perfect copy than ever was extant in the hearts and lives of angels."[146] Christ gave substance to the law, his speech and deeds impeccable manifestations of righteousness: " 'I came not to destroy the law, but to fulfill it.' Yea, and if all the copies of the law that are in the world were burnt, they might be all renewed in his story, insomuch that he is reckoned a new founder of it."[147] Christ clarifies the law of the heart by embodying it in his life.

Third, Goodwin adds that this law is explained in the Scriptures, offering an analogy that links the law of the heart to the original covenant between God and man:

> Yea, and suppose, that covenant (which is the first story and copy of God's will and wisdom) had been utterly lost (like as some of Solomon's books were), yet he by his works of mediation makes a new story of another wisdom infinitely more glorious, viz., the gospel, whereof he is the sole founder, and of whom it is written as being the subject of it. The least line of which is worth all the law, so that the angels stand amazed at the 'treasures of wisdom' that are to found therein, being deeper than ever were revealed in the law.[148]

The imperfections of the law of the heart are clarified further in 1 John 2:8 and the law of Christ in Galatians 6:2. Just as law "came by Moses, but grace and truth by Jesus Christ" (John 1:17), so written revelation subsequently clarified the imperfections previously assigned to laws of the heart. According to Goodwin, new truth clarifies older truth.

Demands Holiness by Uniting With and Controlling Conscience

Concerned with sins committed "against knowledge," Goodwin applies his understanding to links between law and conscience: "When the law, being known, is broken, there is the more contempt

146. V:102.
147. V:102.
148. V:102.

cast upon the law, and the lawgiver also, and so a higher degree of sinning."[149] For support he turns to Numbers 15:30, Job 24:13, and Psalm 50:17; to sin "out of knowledge" (Numbers 15:30) involves directly reproaching the Lord and despising his word; to sin against the light, a metaphor for knowledge is to "rebel" (Job 24:13). The hypocrite, by sinning against knowledge, "casts the law of God behind his back" (Psalm 50:17). Goodwin believes that knowledge of the law is an officer set to see the law "executed and fulfilled," and "makes God present to the conscience," and hence, the law is called a witness (Romans 2:14).[150] Moreover, to sin in the presence of and despite the testimony of this witness is "a higher degree of sinning."[151]

Demands Holiness by Exposing the Totality of Man's Inner Sinful Nature

In Socratic style, Goodwin raises an objection to the law reaching into and controlling all that is in man: "But you will say, Doth the law of God require and command that my nature should be holy?" The answer, predictably, is affirmative. God expressly requires that human nature be holy; the proof text for Goodwin is Leviticus 11: 44–45. As God's nature is, so human nature is commanded to be, added to which is the notion that the "law reacheth to all that is in man"; supporting Goodwin is both Hebrews 4:12 ("for the word of God is quick and powerful, and sharper than any two-edged sword, piercing even to the dividing asunder of soul and spirit, and of the joints and marrow, and is a discerner of the thoughts and intents of the heart")[152] and 1 Thessalonians 5:23 ("And the very God of peace sanctify you wholly: and I pray God your whole spirit, and soul, and body, be preserved blameless unto the coming of our

---

149. IV:168.
150. IV:169.
151. IV:168.
152. X:57.

Lord Jesus Christ.").[153] Antinomians, accepting the Scripture on grace but rejecting the Scripture on law, hold one side of the truth while rejecting the other.[154]

Goodwin defines personal holiness explicitly: "for what is holiness but the law of God written in the heart, the real living law?" In Romans 7:23, this is called the "law of the mind." The law of the mind is contrary to the original corruption afflicting man, called the law of the members. These war against the law of the mind,[155] and in this warfare, sin may "take occasion" because of the commandment (the commandment "thou shalt not" may actually aggravate and excite sin).[156] Further, the laws of the Gentiles communicate that they know, by observation and experience, that man is corrupt by nature.[157]

Demands Holiness by Demanding Satisfaction for Violations

God's holiness, personally offended by violations of his law, must be satisfied to make way for our fellowship with him. Goodwin explores the nature of satisfaction necessary for violations of God's law. According to Psalm 119:126, the offense is itself an effort to destroy the law—"They have willingly destroyed thy law." The offense cannot change the law but can destroy its observance. The measure of satisfaction is determined by the "worth of the law, and of every iota of it, which sin doth what in it lies to make void and of none effect":[158]

> Now seeing satisfaction is *redditio aequicalentis pro aequicalenti*; that which is given in way of restitution must be of an equivalent worth to that which is endamaged; what therefore can any mere creature have to render to God, equivalent to this his law? For is not the least tittle

153. X:58.
154. IV:277.
155. X:57.
156. X:60.
157. X:46.
158. V:84–85.

of the law worth heaven and earth, and so all in it, even saints and all, because God's prerogative lies at stake in it?[159]

Goodwin develops the concept of law being the measure of satisfaction:

> Is it not the *regula*, the pattern, yea, the original copy of all the grace which the saints have? For all grace is but the copy of the law. And doth it not command all that is in them? According to Goodwin, the law determines the work of grace.[160]

The law of God informs grace of the need for it, directs grace to meet the need, and provides the standard to which grace must conform. In simpler terms, the law outlines the problem of sin and grace "reads" the outline, and provides the solution.

Demands Holiness Through Evangelical Faith and Repentance

Goodwin uses the devices of rhetoric to explore the relation of evangelical faith to biblical law. To his Socratic question "whensoever God cometh to work faith in any man's heart, what doth he?" the answer is a conflation of two texts, Galatians 2:19-20 and Romans 7. In the former, "I through the law am dead to the law," Goodwin remarks on the juxtaposition. If anyone "living should have gone to heaven," says Goodwin, it was Paul.[161] His theological pedigree and external conformity to Pharisaic codes were his link with life, rendering him "alive" in his own estimation. In his unconverted state, Paul's perception of biblical law yielded a false security, because by absorption in the Judaistic externals, Paul truncated the significance of biblical law, as his soliloquy reminds us: "I went upon a mistake . . . I thought I should have been saved by my works, by doing: Do this and live. I was mistaken; I saw the law did nothing but condemn me, and that all my works were dead

159. V:85.
160. V:85.
161. I:442.

works; the commandment came, came in the spiritual knowledge of it." Additionally, there is Romans 7, "I was alive, without the law once, but when the commandment came," (Goodwin interjects his own interpretive words at this point, "and arrested me") "sin revived and I died: and the commandment, that was ordained to life, I found to be unto death." According to Goodwin, Paul saw, not the Pharisaic midrash he had substituted for the spiritual content of the law, but the "spiritual holiness the law required." When the commandment "came" to Paul, he was struck "stark dead." (Goodwin illustrates the coming of the commandment as the sun coming into a dark house.)[162]

Goodwin elaborates on the significance of the metonymy "dead" (Romans 7 and Galatians 2:19-20),[163] since to him "dead" means free of all self-approbation, self-aggrandizement, and "self-flattery." The law, in Goodwin's view, is the destroyer of narcissism. People may, because of their naturally deceptive and proud nature, understand that in regard to "whatsoever the word saith," that "he is a living man."[164] Paul lost this natural "self-flattery" when "he was struck of his," and "lay stark dead." Paul understood the law of God in a way that was new. This understanding resulted in change—Paul's understanding of himself in Galatians 2 is different from that which is in Romans 7. By this point (Romans 7:15-25), Paul's confusion had lifted—he realized that "if any man in the world went to hell, he should."[165] As Goodwin postulates, "to work this, to kill a natural man thus, that is alive through self-flattery, and to lay him for dead, it is a mighty work." The reason that Goodwin calls this work mighty is that every man has "self-love in him." Since this is deeply rooted in man's nature, it will never die of its own accord; it must be killed by some powerful external force. Of natural "self-flattery's" refusal to die, Goodwin says "it will never give up the ghost of itself."[166] The old nature possesses a

162. I:443
163. I:442-3.
164. I:442.
165. I:443.
166. I:443.

fury of reason: "all the reason a man hath will fight for arguments to prove himself a living man." The law responds to each of these arguments and puts them to silence (*cf.* Rom. 3:19–20).

Goodwin not only implicates the universality of this natural "self-flattery" but also its duration for all of life: "this same self-flattery, which you are all born with, will struggle for life." This innate desire to praise one's self, to boast in one's attributes and glory in self-deception, is a self-love he calls a "Benjamin," Jacob's most beloved son. Jacob would have sooner died than see any harm to his son. Goodwin defines one's Benjamin as the belief that to think well of one's self is the way to be happy. Jacob said that if Benjamin were killed he would go down to the grave with sorrow, that he would never recover, never have a good day more. So is the attachment of an unregenerate man to his narcissism. "To keep this opinion in a man's heart, that he is a living man, all in a man will fight for it." The role of the law, therefore, is to make man not "think well of" himself, but rather that he is "in a state of damnation." Goodwin says we must "lay the ax to the root of the tree and kill it."[167]

To him the function of the law is to persuade the natural man that he is dead of his sins, and therefore unable to please God. The law renders the sinner dead before God, but this fact needs further illumination. This "mighty work . . . is never thoroughly done till there cometh . . . a spiritual light created in a man's heart,"[168] implying that light is created *in* man not *by* man. This divine illumination is essential if one is to believe that one is "dead." God may "come with terror upon a man's conscience, knock him into a swoon; but self-flattery will revive again when the terrors are off, and he will have a good opinion of himself again." The only means to kill man's self-aggrandizement is the divine impartation of spiritual understanding—"But to kill a man wholly from ever rising again, that a man shall say, as Paul, I am dead to the law for ever, I can never recover this wound, I can never have a good opinion of my former estate more, or of myself more." The spiritual

167. I:443.
168. I:443.

understanding of the law and man's estate (death) are both preparatory to a work of saving grace.[169]

Demands Holiness Through Contemporary Preaching

Goodwin holds that the law must be preached in addition to the Gospel. "And therefore we are feign to make it the greatest of our business to preach the law, and come with that hammer to break your bones in pieces first, that we may then preach the Gospel, as it is Isaiah 62, to the captives, and to bind up the broken-hearted." Goodwin held that preachers should preach both law and the Gospel, and show the connection of one to the other, and how one to the other flows.[170]

CHRIST'S RELATION TO THE LAW OF GOD

The Special Law to Which Christ Conforms

Drawing on John 6:37-40 and 10:15-18, Goodwin contends that Christ holds, over and above the moral law, a special law of love, mercy and pity for sinners. He argues that because the Father gave "Jesus Christ a special command to love sinners," he therefore planted in the heart of Christ a "merciful, gracious disposition" "toward" sinners. Goodwin argues that the twice-repeated phrase "it is my Father's will" implies a specific will. According to Goodwin, a command is "a man's will peremptorily expressed."[171] Because John 10:15-18 refers to the Father's specific will for the Son as a "command," Goodwin argues that three things are both the will and command of the Father: Christ should die for his flock; he receives all that come to him; and he should lose none of those for whom he died, raising them up in the latter day. The testimony of Jesus today, says Goodwin, is the same as it was then: "This

---

169. I:443.
170. V:512.
171. IV:113.

command have I received from my Father, and this is his will" (*cf.* John 10:15–18).¹⁷²

Goodwin enlarges his interpretation of John 6:37–40 and 10:15–18 with two propositions from Psalm 40:8, "I come to do they will, O God" and "Thy law is in my bowels." Because of the unique relationship between the Father and Son, the Father "did put into the heart" of the Son "an instinct of transcendent love." Such a divinely imparted instinct "so strongly inclined him to perform" the Father's will, that Christ "should have no more need of commands." Because this "law" was in Christ's "bowels," Goodwin designates this "instinct of transcendent love," ἀστόργος. Goodwin illustrates this ἀστόργος as an "especial love," like the love God has "put into the hearts of parents towards their own children, more than to all other men's children which they see besides, although more beautiful and more witty than their own." "Thy will" in both Psalm 40:8 and John 6:37–40 Goodwin interprets as a "law," according to John 10:15–18. Citing Colossians 3:12 ("bowels of mercy, kindness"), Goodwin interprets "bowels" as an equivalent expression for the "most tender affections." The literal rendering of Psalm 40:8 is, in Goodwin's translation, "in the midst of my bowels." Hence, the Father's law was "deeply engraven; it had its seat in the center, it sat nearest and was most inward in his heart."¹⁷³

Goodwin elaborates on the nature of this law of transcendent love as written in the depth of Christ's heart, by seeing Christ as the second Adam (*cf.* 1 Corinthians 15:33). Since the first Adam had a special law *non concendi*, over and above the moral law (he was prohibited the tree of knowledge and commanded to multiply and subdue the earth), the second Adam also had a special law *non concendi*, over and above the moral law (compare John 10:15–18).¹⁷⁴ "As God would have us shew love unto him by loving his children, so he would have Christ also shew his love towards him by loving us."¹⁷⁵ Actually, Christ comforts himself in John

172. IV:114.
173. IV:114.
174. IV:114.
175. IV:115.

10:17–18, "Therefore doth my Father love me." This implies that God should love Christ "the better" for the love he shows toward the flock of his believers. Regarding the role of the Father, Goodwin offers a soliloquy: "Son, as you would have my love continue towards you, let me see your love towards me shewn in being kind to these I have given you, 'whom I have loved with the same love wherewith I have loved you,' as you have it" (John 17:23)."[176] The Father himself wrote this law of love in Christ, so it become natural to Christ, "and so indelible, and as other moral laws of God written upon the heart are, perpetual." Goodwin then explores the relationship linking this law of the Father with the love in Christ's heart:

> And as in us, when we shall be in heaven, though faith shall fail and hope vanish, yet love shall continue, as the apostle speaks; so doth this love in Christ's heart continue also, and suffers no decay, and is shewn as much now in revenging sinners and interceding for them, and being spiritual unto them, as then in dying for them. And this love to sinners being so commanded and pressed upon him, as was said, that as he would have his Father love him, he should love them, and so being urged upon all that great love that is between him and his Father, this as it must needs work and boil up a strong love unto sinners, so likewise the most constant and never-decaying love that could be.[177]

Again citing John, this time John 15:10, Goodwin claims this law as a "great tie" between the Father and Son:

> He moveth his disciples to "keep the commandments" he gave them, and useth this argument, "For so shall you abide in my love," and backs it with his own instance, "Even as I have kept my Father's commandments, and abide in his love." Now, therefore, this being the great commandment that God layeth on him, to love and die for, and to continue to love and receive, sinners that come to him, and raise them up at the latter day, certainly

176. IV:115.
177. IV:115.

he continues to keep it most exactly, as being one of the great ties between him and his Father, so to continue in his love to him.[178]

The Perfect Obedience That Christ Rendered

Christ's obedience to the law was complete. In contradistinction, no other creature was capable of offering this:

> And whereas the creatures must have gone over their works again and again to eternity, done nothing but written the blurred copy of their obedience, copy after copy, in their lives, and so have made nothing perfect, there is in Christ a fulfilling of but once by him, which will serve for the eternal debt of active obedience. And as by once offering himself, Hebrews 10:14, so by one righteousness and obedience, Romans 5:18.[179]

Christ told his Father in no uncertain terms that his obedience was complete: "I have finished the work which thou gavest me to do" (John 17:4). Moreover, his death imminent, Christ said to his apostles, that he "had now but one thing to do, and that was to drink of the last cup; and "how do I long," says he, "till it be accomplished!" Christ actively obeyed the law, but also endured its penalty on the cross, since obeying, Christ suffered; in suffering, Christ could obey. In the end Christ could say of both, "It is finished."[180]

For thirty-three years, Christ "fulfilled the law in service" and through "obedience performed" it. "I do always the things that please him" (John 8:29). Further, Christ was "a servant," and "obedient unto death, even the death of the cross" (Philippians 2:8). The nature of Christ's obedience (*cf.* Philippians 2:8) was twofold; the righteousness was sufficient not only for his own standing but

---

178. IV:115.
179. V:133.
180. V:133.

also that of the elect.[181] Thus, Christ's obedience was supererogation—he earned a justified status, like a clean bill of health, for each and every one for whom he lived and died. "My servant shall justify many" (Isaiah 53). Thus, Christ's service was not only for himself but others. As a man Christ submitted to the law, but did so as a man personally united to the Godhead; in partaking of all sovereign endowments, he is both subject to, and Lord of, the law (*cf.* Matthew 22:18). Christ's submission to the law is "truly the obedience of God." The active obedience of Christ is the righteousness of God; the passive obedience of Christ is the blood, the sacrifice of God (*cf.* Acts 20:28). Jehovah himself, who had no need for acquired righteousness, nonetheless acquired righteousness for us, but it is through the obedience of the Son of God that the elect have a source of righteousness (Jeremiah 23:6).[182]

The Perfect Satisfaction That He Earned

Goodwin develops in a dialogue the interaction of Christ and the law:

> What the law saith, it saith it to sinners. Well, let the law say what it will, Christ answers it. It says, You are a sinner. Well, but Jesus Christ was made sin for me. You are under the curse. True, but Jesus Christ was made a curse for me, that I might be made the righteousness of God in him. Goodwin proceeds to outline the three aspects of justification—first, that sin is taken away. Second, that we have actual righteousness reckoned to us. But third, Goodwin explains that the law is not yet fulfilled in the former two elements because we have "corruption of nature in us." To Goodwin, Christ came, according to Romans 8:4, into the world in a human nature, "and fulfilled the righteousness of the law, in having that nature perfectly holy." Goodwin sees this threefold justification as "perfect justification."[183]

181. V:131.
182. V:132.
183. V:352.

He holds that the "ends and grounds of giving God's law were to declare and shew forth his justice, and hatred against sin wherever he found it." The law is a testimony of God's thoughts and feelings toward sin. Although the law stipulates God's hatred of the sin of man, Goodwin explains God's refraining from the prerogative of anger:

> Neither is the party to be satisfied wronged, if he that undertakes it be of ability fully to satisfy and to fulfill what he requires, and if being the lawgiver, he be willing to assent to this act of his, and to accept it. For, being Lord of his own law, he may dispense with the letter of it, if so be those holy ends, which counsel had in making it, be accomplished and attained; and if the reason of the law and lawgiver be satisfied, then is the law.[184]

In other words, the Lawgiver can determine the penalties attached to his own law according to his own pleasure. This Lawgiver prerogative allows him to place the penalty of the law upon Christ the Mediator, rather than on the law-breakers.

Citing an unnamed ancient, Goodwin says "neither against the law nor according to the law; but above the law and for the sake of the law," referring to the Mediator's role:

> And although the law doth not mention or name a surety, and the malefactor's single bond be only mentioned therein, and the threatening directed against him, and his name is only in the project, because the law in itself supposeth as yet none else quietly, and can challenge none else, yet if some other, that is lord of his own action, subject himself to the law willingly, which will of his is a law to him, and the lawgiver himself, that is of the law, accepts this, as seeing the same ends shall be satisfied for which he made the law; in this case the law takes hold of the surety or undertaker, and he may let the malefactor go free.[185]

---

184. V:18.
185. V:18.

Goodwin holds that if the "lawgiver be willing" to divert punishments to a "surety," he may do so because "he is lord of his own law." Nonetheless, he must fulfill "those holy ends which his counsel had in making it."[186] Goodwin argues, therefore, that it is not the law itself that the Lawgiver renders of no effect, but rather the penalty that he dispenses in a manner pleasing to himself.

Christ's work, in the words of Goodwin, was "enough to stop the law's mouth." Defiantly, Goodwin challenges the law: "let the law... into open court." When the mock court subpoenas the law for its charges against Christ, Goodwin, personifying the law in the feminine gender, says, "she returns answer, that she hath it not; we find then that it is 'taken out of the way' " (Colossians 2:14). The law's charges against the Mediator and all the elect under his mediatorship are expunged (Colossians 2:14). Goodwin explains "how and by whom" these charges are extinguished—they are not removed "surreptitiously, and by stealth, or by force and violence," but rather they are relinquished legally and openly in the face of the court of justice. Christ himself "blotted out" the charges, nailed them to his cross, thus "triumphing openly" over them. The moral law was a creditor, to which all mankind was a debtor. Further, the Jews were debtors who were obliged to fulfill the whole written law. "He that is circumcised is a debtor to the whole law." But once the debt was paid by Christ, the law "hath nothing to shew against believers so as to condemn us." Goodwin parallels the comprehensive and exhaustive nature of the law's demands with the purity and righteousness of Christ:

> But yet if the law, or any legal conscience, would notwithstanding have further satisfaction, and put us to prove and shew how the particular debts due thereunto were paid and discharged, both that of service to be done, and fulfilling all the law, by active obedience, and then by passive obedience also, and know how the punishment and curse threatened was undergone, the particular discharge is yet upon record. Christ hath done both fully; and what he hath done and suffered hath that which the

---

186. V:490.

obedience and sufferings of no pure creature could have ... done.[187]

Christ's satisfaction was thorough, as Goodwin personifies the law: "now we have shown such abundant satisfaction given to God in point of his honour, the law methinks may well sit down and never so much as mention the debt that is its due."[188] Although "the law" is satisfied by Christ's sacrifice on the cross, Goodwin adds, "Yet if the law will needs bring in her bill also, there will be found satisfaction full enough for its claim also."[189]

Goodwin reminds us that Christ "was made sin and a curse for us, because he, redeeming us who were under the law, must become that which we were in the account and judgment of the law." Goodwin cites Galatians 4:4–5, "God sent his Son, made under the law, to redeem them that are under the law." Arguing from this example, Goodwin states that Christ redeemed us from the law by having made it. "He that made the law, was made under it for us." Although "both he and we were under the law; but with this difference, we were born under it, but he was made under it, by a voluntary covenant freely undergoing it." The phrase "under the law" Goodwin defines as being "subject to all that the law is able to say or do." (The same phrase is used in Romans 3:19, "What the law says, it says unto them that are under the law.") Thus, whoever is under the law, the law is able to say and exact of him whatever it says and requires. As Christ became an "undertaker," one who undertook obedience to the law, "the law has as much to say to him as unto sinners themselves."[190]

CONCLUSION

Not only does Goodwin possess keen insights into theological law, but he communicates them convincingly, using Socratic dialogue

---

187. V:131.
188. V:131.
189. V:131.
190. V:180.

to highlight arguments. At times he steps back from dogma and states, "So I have observed."[191] None of Goodwin's statements, however, would identify him as a "theonomist" or a non-theonomist. Modern debates notwithstanding, Goodwin's depth of perception illumines the Reformed churches with a brightness rare in our dark day.

---

191. V:55.

STEPHEN CHARNOCK'S VIEW OF SUBSTANTIVE BIBLICAL LAW

Stephen Charnock (1628-80), chaplain to Henry Cromwell, the governor of Ireland, and joint pastor with Thomas Watson at Crosby Hall, published only one sermon in his lifetime. The extent of his posthumous publications belies the impact of his ministry, since his preaching, without notes, distinguishes him for both erudition and clarity. Furthermore, his theological expertise led to a fellowship at New College, Oxford, where he associated with the Puritans Thomas Goodwin and John Howe.[1] His works were published posthumously in the 1680s, his complete works reprinted in nine volumes in 1815. In 1869, Nichol published Charnock's works in five volumes.

Charnock's theology of the law of God is contained in the 19th chapter of the Westminster Confession of Faith of 1648, and in questions 91-150 of the Larger Catechism. No better summary of Charnock's thought exists that the seven theses of the Westminster Confession on the law of God.[2] Contained in Nichol's *Complete Works of Stephen Charnock*, Charnock's references to God's law of God may be examined according to three foci—the relation of the law of God to God's divine nature, the relation of the law

---

1. Stephen Charnock, *Christ Crucified* (Lynchburg: James Family Publications, n. d.), forward by Ed Hindson.

2. The Confession of Faith. The Larger and Shorter Catechisms, with the Scripture Proofs at Large: Together with the Sum of Saving Knowledge. (Glasgow: Free Presbyterian Publications, 1985), pp. 79-84, 91-150.

of God to Christ the Mediator, and relation of the law of God to mankind.

THE RELATION OF THE LAW OF GOD TO GOD'S NATURE

The Relation of the Law of God to God's Incommunicable Attributes

The Relation of the Law of God to God's Sovereignty

In one short section of his works, Charnock describes the relationship of God's law to his sovereignty. God's law reveals his unhindered, unrestricted authority; for some of God's laws there is no reason than this: that God wills it so.[3] These laws, in which Charnock includes Genesis 2:17 ("not eating of the tree of the knowledge of good and evil") are based solely on divine prerogatives:

> No other reason of this seems to us, but a resolve to try man's obedience in a way of absolute sovereignty, and to manifest his right over all creatures, to reserve what he pleased to himself, and permit the use of what he pleased to man, and to signify to man that he was to depend on him, who was his Lord, and not on his own will.[4]

The law of God, therefore, issues from the Sovereign, who has the right to demand what he will from his creatures. Mankind has no claims upon God; only God possesses full claims upon mankind (*cf.* Romans 9:19–21).

---

3. Stephen Charnock, *The Existence and Attributes of God* (Grand Rapids: Baker Book House, 1979), I:69. All subsequent citations conform to the following forms: (1) Volume numbers "I" and "II" cite either of the two volumes of Stephen Charnock, *The Existence and Attributes of God* (Grand Rapids: Baker Book House, 1979); (2) Citations including volume numbers "III," "IV," and "V," originate from Stephen Charnock, *The Complete Works of Stephen Charnock, B. D.* (Edinburgh: James Nichol, 1865).

4. II:389.

THE PURITAN VIEW OF SUBSTANTIVE BIBLICAL LAW

The Relation of the Law of God to God's Majesty

Although all of God's laws reflect his attributes, Charnock sees particularly in the character of the decalogue a reflection of his majesty. Exodus 31:18 testifies to this attribute as does no other part of the law (the divine finger writing upon "tables of stone"). Although Moses recorded the law on tables of stone, the law itself was generated by God alone, for his own purposes, as Charnock reminds us (Exodus 32:16): "And the tables were the work of God, and the writing was the writing of God engraven upon the tables." Furthermore, God endeavored to have his sovereignty "eminently appear" through the attendance by his "heavenly militia" (Deuteronomy 32:2). This law is called a "fiery law . . . coming from his right hand." Thus, Charnock concludes that it was "published with all the marks of supreme majesty."[5] One aspect of the law, therefore, is its reflection of the unique majesty of God.

The Relation of the Law of God to God's Spirituality

Charnock distinguishes the law of God from the law of mankind by pointing out that God's law manages the conscience, this capacity a manifestation of God's spiritual character. The law touches the human spirit, which includes the conscience, as Charnock elaborates:

> God hath given man but an authority over the half of man, and the worst half too, that which is of an earthly original; but reserved the authority over the better and more heavenly half to himself. The dominion of earthly princes extends only to the bodies of men; they have no authority over the soul, their punishment and rewards cannot reach it; and therefore their laws, by their single authority, cannot bind it, but as they are coincident with the law of God.[6]

---

5. II:390.
6. II:391.

Since only God may judge the conscience (Luke 12:3-4), judging is his province only. Only he can impose the laws that govern its working. The nature of conscience, as part of the human spirit, interrelates with the law of God:

> It is out of the reach of human penal authority... Conscience is a book in some sort as sacred as the Scripture; no addition can be lawfully made to it, no subtraction from it. Men cannot diminish the duty of conscience, or raze out the law God hath stamped upon it. They cannot put a *supersedes* to the writ of conscience, or stop its mouth with a *noli prosequi*. They can make no addition by their authority to bind it; it is a flower in the crown of Divine sovereignty only.[7]

The Relation of the Law of God to God's Immutability

What Charnock sets out to demonstrate is that a change of God's law does not imply a change in God himself. Further, a change in God's law does not imply the existence of more than one God. Using two analogies, Charnock explains the changes in God's laws: first, young children should be dealt with differently from adults (*cf.* Galatians 4:3). Second, a physician's skill is not questionable if he prescribes a remedy for one malady but a different one for another malady.[8]

Charnock argues that it is the province of God to dispense with his own laws, whether they be over nature or men. God exercises his right to govern the laws of nature by arresting the law of physics to produce miracles—"to make the sun stand still, or move backward, to bind up the womb of the earth, and bar the influences of the clouds, bridle the rage of the fire, and the fury of lions; make the liquid waters stand like a wall, or pull up the dam, which he hath set to the sea, and command it to overflow the neighboring

---

7. II:391.
8. II:346.

countries."⁹ Over mankind, God has the right to dispense with his own laws, a phenomenon that causes Charnock to comment on the transformation of the ceremonial law into something higher. God transformed Old Testament ceremonial religion by destroying the externals, the Temple and its priesthood, lifting it to a higher, more spiritual plane. Charnock does not comment on the Old Testament case laws and their penalties, or mention them as being transformed, though his development of the continuity of the law implies a belief in the abiding validity of case laws and their penalties (but not the ceremonial laws). His sense of an abiding validity of judicial law is within the parameter of the Westminster Confession's phraseology—"general equity."[10]

The Relation of the Law of God to God's Communicable Attributes

The Relation of the Law of God to God's Wisdom

God's laws reflect both a divine and human *telos*. "An universal wisdom and righteousness glitters in the Divine law." The law reflects the superiority of God—"who teaches like God?" (Job 36:22).[11] Not only do they reflect God's authority, because of his glory, but they disclose his wisdom "respecting mankind's benefit." God's law perfects man's nature by conferring wisdom upon him—the law "enlightens the eyes" (Psalm 19:7–8). Thus law imparts a twofold knowledge, both of God and self.

Charnock declaims the propriety of God's law by identifying the consequences of its absence. It is this absence that turns people into beasts.[12] The laws of men are "often unjust, oppressive, cruel, sometimes against the law of nature."[13] On the contrary, the Israelite nation, through the benefit of biblical law, would have all

9. II:391–92.
10. II:392.
11. II:528.
12. II:527.
13. II:528.

citizens be "statesmen" as to judicial matters, "ecclesiastics" as to ceremonial matters, and "honest men" in economic matters. Furthermore, Charnock praises biblical law because it was designed not for one particular nation, but to accommodate all mankind, "in the variety of climates and countries wherein they live." The results of mankind's total obedience to God's law would be stupendous:

> And if [the law were][14] well observed, [it] would alter the face of the world, and make it look with another hue. The world would be altered from a brutish to a human world; it would change lions and wolves, men of lion-like and wolfish disposition, into reason and sweetness. And because the whole law is summed up in love, it obligeth us to endeavor the preservation of one another's beings, the favoring of one another's interests, and increasing the goods, as much as justice will permit, and keeping up one another's credits, because love, which is the soul of the law, is not shown by a cessation from action, but signifies an ardor, upon all occasion, in doing good. I say, were this well observed, the world would be another thing than it is: it would become a religious fraternity; the voice of enmity, and the noise of groans and cursing, would not be heard in our streets; peace would be in all borders; plenty of charity in the midst of cities and countries; joy and singing would sound in all habitations.[15]

Universal obedience to God's law would, therefore, transmit the blessedness of his wisdom to the whole earth.

The Relation of the Law of God to God's Mercy

Moreover, God cannot impose injurious laws—to do so would dishonor himself. God's nature compels his law to be true, not false, because God is truth; to be beneficial, not injurious, because God is good; and profitable, not vain, because God is wise. Giving three illustrations, Charnock pleads us to submit to God's laws: Noah

14. Brackets added for clarity.
15. II:527.

submitted and thus saved the human race; the children of Israel submitted and invaded the land and thus saved the Messianic seed; and the Savior submitted to the law of God, and saved the elect.[16] In these instances, the law of God transmits God's mercy to mankind, if they obey.

The Relation of the Law of God to God's Holiness

Charnock develops the theme of the relationship between the law of God and God's holiness in these parts—a theodicy for the institution of a law God knew would be disobeyed; an exposure of the sin of charging the law with rigidity; and a discussion of the significance of the law's penalties. A common objection to God's institution of the law is "Why would he institute a law he knew men would not obey?" "Is this a blemish to his holiness?" To these questions, Charnock answers: (1) "The Scripture frees God fully from any blame in this, and lays it wholly upon Satan, as the tempter, and upon man, as the determiner of his own will (Genesis 3:6)." Charnock lifts from God responsibility for man's disobedience in Eden, shifting it to Satan and mankind. (2) Charnock argues that man was created with original uprightness (according to Ecclesiastes 7:29); therefore the divine character cannot be faulted if the creature, of the creature's own power and accord, corrupted himself. Charnock makes his point with the following illustration: silver, gold, and other metals were originally created by God as pure of "form and figure," but the metals are capable of other forms, as the result of efforts of men. Charnock is saying that mankind in his original state took another form because of Satan's temptation. He adds other analogs—an excellent instrument, framed by a skilled craftsman, may easily be marred by a careless hand. Further, the workman who built the house "strong" and with "good posture" should not be impugned if the house be ruined through wastefulness or carelessness.

---

16. II:604.

STEPHEN CHARNOCK'S VIEW OF SUBSTANTIVE BIBLICAL LAW

In no uncertain terms, Charnock equates charging the law of God with rigidity as "contemning the holiness of God." When men complain that the law "shackles" them, and "prohibits their desired pleasures," they "cast dirt upon the holiness of God." The reason for the Israelites' hatred of the prophets, according to Charnock, was their hatred of the law.[17] Further, the rebellious Israelites attempted to sway the prophets from their calling, calling them to "get out of the way," and turn aside out of the path, and cause the Holy One of Israel to cease from before them (Isaiah 30:10–11).[18] Charnock does not waste sympathy on backsliding Israelites:

> Let him [God] be gone from us, since he will not countenance our vices, and indulge our crimes; we would rather hear there is a God, than thou would tell us of a holy one. We are contrary to the law, when we wish it were not so exact; and therefore, contrary to the holiness of God, which set the stamp of exactness and righteousness upon it. We think him injurious to our liberty, when by his precept he thwarts our pleasure; we wish it of another frame, more milked, more suitable to our minds; it is the same, as if we should openly blame God for consulting with his own righteousness, and not with our humors, before he settled his law; that he should not have drawn from the depths of his righteous nature, but squared it to accommodate our corruption.[19]

God's holiness, according to Charnock, is manifested in the penalties inflicted for violations. The penalties for destroying God's law imply the interrelationship of divine holiness and justice. The root of God's holiness is God's justice, just as the triumph of God's holiness is God's justice. According to Charnock, both of these attributes are circumscribed in one term, "righteousness." Citing Psalm 103:6 ("The Lord executeth righteousness and judgment for all that are oppressed.") and Daniel 9:7 ("Righteousness [that is justice] belongeth to thee"), Charnock explains that holiness and

---

17. II:178.
18. II:178–79.
19. II:179. The contents of the brackets were added for clarity.

justice, subsumed under divine righteousness, are responsible for "all the tempests and storms in the world." One penalty for sin was the overthrowing of the Jewish state. Divine righteousness hardened the hearts of the unbelieving Jews and "cashiered a nation, once dear to him, from the honor of his protection." Despite this act of reprobation, God's holiness is applauded by the seraphim (Isaiah 6:3, *cf.* 9–11).[20] (This penalty for disobeying God's law was prophesied in Deuteronomy 28:15ff.)

The Relation of the Law of God to God's Goodness

The law of God, according to Charnock, manifests the goodness of God. The same divine goodness that motivated creation motivated God to govern by his law. If God had left mankind without law, God would cease to be good, according to Charnock,[21] since God's goodness in government appears in his "fitting the law to the nature of man."[22] In man's original condition, man was "upright" (Ecclesiastes 7:29), and therefore able to keep the Edenic law. The Edenic law was "rather below than above his strength." The law was suited to his nature and his nature to the law. They were like "exact straight lines, touching one another in every part when joined together." Intellectually, volitionally, and emotionally, man's original nature was suited to the law: "it was not above his understanding to know it, nor his will to embrace it nor his passions to be regulated by it." God required of man no more than was already written in the heart of man, in his original state (*cf.* Romans 2:15). The nature of the moral law, as written in the heart, was not grievous (1 John 5:3), coming not only from the authority of a sovereign but from the goodness of a father.

Moreover, in his original state mankind would respond to the moral law with pleasure, "a delightful satisfaction." Obeying the moral law, as written in the heart, would produce "extraordinary

20. II:132.
21. II:252.
22. II:252.

contentment." As with the original nature of man, the renewed regenerate nature of fallen man finds in the law of God a "suitableness which kindles delight" (Psalm 1:2). To both the original and renewed natures of mankind, the law is neither a shock nor a burden.[23] Rather, the divine goodness which shines in it prompts praise to the Lawgiver (*cf.* Psalm 119:164).[24]

For not only does the law of God suit the nature of mankind, it also suits his happiness. Divine goodness cannot, by its very nature, impose that which is unreasonable, oppressive, or uncomfortable. "Bitterness cannot come from that which is altogether sweet." Because the Lawgiver is both infinitely wise and good, his commandments are both rational and beneficial. Charnock describes the divine Lawgiver as an excellent prince, who will make laws not only for his own honor but for his people's good. Scripture emphasizes that God's law is "for our good" (Deuteronomy 10:12–13). God never pleaded with the Israelites to obey his law on account of his divine authority; rather God pleaded with them to obey because it was in their best interest (Deuteronomy 4:40; 12:28). "Great peace" have they which observe God's law. Whenever the Israelites fell from God's law, he grieved for their impairment of their own felicity—"Oh, that thou hast hearkened to my commandments! Then had thy peace been as a river!" (Isaiah 48:18).[25] The objective of the law was eternal life, according to Christ in his dialogue with the rich young ruler. Had Adam obeyed the moral law written upon his heart, he would have attained eternal life; thus Charnock sees the original Edenic law as the conditional covenant of works. In the same vein, the martyr Stephen refers to the law given to Moses as the "living oracles" (Acts 7:38).[26] Charnock explores the intent of God:

> The chief design of God in his law is the happiness of the subject; an obedience is intended by him as a means for the attaining of happiness, as well as preserving his

---

23. II:252.
24. II:253.
25. II:253.
26. II:253–54.

own sovereignty: this is the reason why he wished that Israel had walked in his way, "that their time might have endured forever" (Ps. 81:13, 15, 16). And by the same reason, this was his intendment in his law given to man, and his covenant made with man at the creation, that he might be fed with the finest part of his bounty, and be satisfied with honey out of the eternal Rock of Ages.[27]

Not only does God grant mankind a benevolent law but by his goodness encourages obedience. Rather than simply command obedience that is predicated upon his lordship, God motivates his hearers to obedience by promises of bounty and rewards.[28] Charnock calls these "arguments of sweetness," since by these gentle overtures, God attracts people to their duties.[29] Charnock observes that the nature of man is managed according to two responses—hope and fear. The divine Lawgiver utilizes both to inspire obedience. God uses hope to hold before men the rewards of a blessing, if they obey; he uses fear to threaten punishment. It is through the elevation of hope and the excitement of fear that God inspires us to our greatest happiness.[30]

Not only by threats and punishments, but also by benefiting does God inspire us to obey. The benefits God bestowed upon the Israelites by bringing them up from bondage (Isaiah 2:2 and Jeremiah 11:7–8) conveys the "strong obligations to an ingenuous observance" of the law.[31] "God can enjoin the observance of nothing but what is good."[32] Charnock interprets 1 John 5:3 ("his commands are not grievous") as not "grievous in their nature" nor "grievous to one possessed with a true reason."[33]

---

27. II:253–54.
28. II:254.
29. II:255.
30. II:255.
31. II:339.
32. II:339.
33. II:339.

THE RELATION OF THE LAW OF GOD TO CHRIST THE MEDIATOR

Christ honored the law of God in both its precept and penalty. Charnock describes the law as honorable and righteous in both its precept and penalty. In the Garden, for example, the precept was obedience. Since God intended that people should obey, he added a penalty for disobedience. Although obedience was the design, God added a penalty to enforce the authority of the precept. After the fall, God-given laws still have both precept, designed for man's obedience, and penalty, designed for man's correction (Genesis 2:17).[34] Both precept and penalty honor God's attributes. The holiness of God is honored in the obedience of the precept; the justice of God is honored by the execution of the penalty.

This law was vindicated by Christ's own obedience. He vindicated the precepts of the law by conforming to it; he vindicated the notion of penalty by the manner of his dying. Christ exactly performed the precepts, and upon him the curse was "punctually executed." Through voluntarily observing precepts, and voluntarily undergoing the penalty, Christ, the Wisdom of God (*cf.* Proverbs 9), vindicated the holiness of God as expressed by the precept and justice of God.[35]

THE RELATION OF THE LAW OF GOD TO THE THREEFOLD STATE OF MAN—ORIGINAL, FALLEN, AND REGENERATE

The Relation of the Law of God to the Original State of Man

The rule of God's law extends to the whole universe, his sovereignty allowing him to enact laws for the whole universe, including the heavens, angels, mankind, and beasts. Even the "heavens have their ordinances" (Job 38:33).[36] Angels who fell into sin must

---

34. II:565.
35. II:566.
36. II:389.

have violated some law because where there is no law, there is no transgression. Charnock postulates that this law was a moral law that accorded with their spiritual natures: "a love to God, a worship of him, and a love to one another in their societies and persons."[37] Men are under the law of God because:

> Every son of Adam, at his coming into the world, brings with him a law in his nature, and when reason clears itself up from the clouds of sense, he can make some difference between good and evil; discern something fit and just. Every man finds a law within him that checks him if he offends it; none are without a legal indictment and a legal executioner within them.[38]

Even beasts are ruled by an unwritten law of divine providence; this governing of unintelligent life is in a "manner inferior to the rule of man."[39] Clearly, God's law extends to the whole universe.

Charnock later argues that men should imitate God's holiness because it is within man's created nature to do so. Man's nature, which is in the image of God, includes a natural urge to resemble God. In man's original state, this righteous nature included desire to resemble God in his purity, rather than his knowledge (Genesis 3:5). Had there been no desire by man to resemble God's holiness, the devil's attempts to confuse man, by resembling God in knowledge, rather than holiness, would have been "as an arrow shot against a brazen wall." In the fall, man "mistook the term," incorrectly thinking that he could resemble God in knowledge, and not purity.[40]

---

37. II:388–89.
38. II:388.
39. II:389.
40. II:200.

STEPHEN CHARNOCK'S VIEW OF SUBSTANTIVE BIBLICAL LAW

The Relation of the Law of God to the Fallen State of Man

In Charnock's view, the fallen nature of man and spiritual nature of the law are in a constant state of enmity, because law is spiritual and man carnal (Romans 7:14), both are opposed to each other. For peace to prevail, one of the parties must change. The law has no friendship towards man, or vice versa, since their natures are so contrary. What the law commands is disgusting to the flesh, what the flesh desires is displeasing to the law.[41]

To Charnock, the existence of human moral awareness is everywhere evident. He argues that "there is a notion of good and evil in the consciences of men" which "evidences" itself in "laws that are common to all countries." These laws serve three purposes: (1) the preservation of their societies, (2) discouragement of vice, and (3) encouragement of virtue.

Supposing that laws common to all nations must originate from a common source, Charnock concludes that this common standard is founded upon "common reason." Since Paul presupposes that a civil magistrate is a minister of God for good, hence a commonly accepted good, such a perception must issue from "common reason" (Romans 13:1). Moreover, since all nations "do by nature things contained in the law" (Romans 2:14), there must be a natural "common reason."[42] Charnock argues for the existence of "common reason" on the following grounds: (1) There are natural principles within mankind which incline him to distinguish between good and evil. "How would this be if there were not some rule in him to distinguish good and evil?" Charnock argues to the contrary by supposition. If there were no common reason, there is simply no other way men would know good from evil, and since men know good from evil, this common reason exists. (2) If there were no "common reason, "Charnock deduces "there would be no sin" (citing 1 John 3:4, because "where there is no law there is no transgression"). Since God holds men responsible for sin, and God is not unjust, there must be some law telling man of his sin, since

---

41. *The Complete Works of Charnock*, III:34.
42. I:69.

by law is sin known (*cf.* Romans 3:20–21). (3) If there were no innate reason, why do men condemn evil in themselves and others, when their own inner natures are depraved? Thus, there is some component, operating within man's psyche, that distinguishes good from evil.[43] (4) The extent of such differentiation is universal. Everyone can discern good from evil, and since all, not some, do so there must be a natural component causing such actions, because universal effects require universal causes.[44] Charnock further develops his doctrine of "common reason" by identifying its source. Since every law has a lawgiver, common reason must have a lawgiver. The lawgiver cannot be man himself, because man's corrupt nature diminishes his moral sensibilities—thus, the lawgiver must be God.[45]

Charnock compares the light of the moral law, as written upon man's heart, with the light derived from Scripture. The former is likened to starlight (which may be sufficient to reveal the "greatness of the filth of sin"), but the written law of God is bright enough to examine heart's "little sprouts and branches of sin."[46] Thus, both common reason and the written law of God expose the sins of fallen man.

Charnock further comments on man's response to God's law. Arguing from Romans 2:14 ("the Gentiles do, by nature, the things contained in the law"), Charnock states there is affinity between God's law and man's reason, since from the law emerges a natural beauty which "darts" upon the reasons and consciences of men. Conscience then dictates that God's law is worthy of obedience; even if men do not practice the law, they yet apprehend its correctness.

In another vein, God's law commends itself to the consciences of men. The law is "goodness at the root, not only in action, but affection; not only in motion of the members, but the disposition of

---

43. I:69.
44. I:70.
45. I:70.
46. IV:177.

the soul."[47] Exploring the response of men to God's law, Charnock explains the exclusive nature of divine law. "It is treason in any against the crown of God, to mint laws with a stamp contrary to that of heaven, whereby they renounce their due subjection, and vie with God for dominion, snatch the supremacy from him, and account themselves more lords than the Sovereign Monarch of the world." Charnock's monarchs are not without flaws:

> When men will not let God be the judge of good and evil, but put in their own vote, controlling his to establish their own; such are not content to be as gods, subordinate to the supreme God, to sit at his feet; nor co-ordinate with him, to sit equal upon his throne; but paramount to him, to over-top and shadow his crown;—a boldness that leaves the serpent, in the first temptation, under the character of a more commendable modesty.[48]

When men make additions to God's laws, they malign the sovereignty of God. "The authority of a sovereign Lawgiver is invaded and maligned when an inferior presumes to make order equivalent to his edicts."[49] When men obey earthly rulers before God, be they servants, employees, or citizens, they set man upon the throne of God, and God at "the footstool of man; to set man above, and God beneath; to make him the tail, and not the head, as God speaks in another case of Israel (Deuteronomy 28:13)."[50]

Man should not tamper with God's laws, but revere them. Because God the Lawgiver is infinitely wise, disputes against his "precepts and methods" are intolerable. Should the wisdom of God's precepts and methods be beyond man's reasoning, then they should entertain them with respect and reverence, nonetheless.[51] Charnock compares the reverence one displays toward the law of God with the respect accorded a prince; man should not tamper with God's laws.

47. IV:529.
48. II:431.
49. II:432–434.
50. II:434.
51. II:603–604.

> We must not think to mend our Creator's laws, and presume to judge and condemn his righteous statutes. If the flesh rise up in opposition, we must cross its motions, and silence its murmurings.[52]

Charnock also develops his commentary on the importance of the law in conversion. By itself, the law cannot save souls; rather the law leads men to Christ by exposing their need of him. "The law will instruct, not heal. It acquaints us with our duty, not our remedy; it vitiates sin, not allays it; it exasperates our venom, but doth not tame it; though it shews man his miserable condition, yet a man by it doth not gain one drop of repentance. It tells us what we should do, but corrects not the enmity of our nature whereby we may do it."[53]

The Relation of the Law of God to the Regenerate State of Man

Charnock's treatment of the relation of the law of God and the new nature includes a differentiation of the natural law of nature and the new regenerate mind, the regenerate nature's responses to the law, and elements of the law to which the regenerate nature is accountable. Charnock distinguishes the law of nature and the law of God in the regenerate mind. The two are in agreement, but the former is natural, originating in the covenant of works; the latter originates in the Spirit of God.[54] The new nature is created by God, κτίσθεντα, implying it is a re-creation of the original nature that was lost by Adam through the fall.[55] God's law, pertaining to the new nature, is written in the heart (2 Corinthians 3:3).[56] The heart's law applies to inward man, according to Psalm 119:9, "thy word have I hid in my heart, that I might not sin against thee,"

---

52. II:604.
53. IV:202.
54. IV:119.
55. IV:119.
56. IV:120.

and Jeremiah 31:32, "thy word will I write upon the heart."[57] The new nature includes an inner ability to know and obey the law,[58] an inward conformity to the law,[59] a mighty affection for the law,[60] and a strong propensity to obedience.[61] A believer's relationship to the law is that of a subject to its "preceptive and minatory part" (that is, its precepts and penalties).[62]

Charnock discusses not only the character of man's regenerate nature in relation to the law but the overall purpose of the regenerate nature, which is conformity to the holiness of the law. According to Charnock, believers must labor to conform with the holiness of God (*cf.* 1 Peter 1:15, 16). The nature of God as presented in the Scriptures provides a template for man to copy, and also a motive, that might persuade believers to holiness (1 John 3:3; Matthew 5:48; Leviticus 11:44; 1 Peter 1:15-16). Charnock emphasizes that the pattern given us is not the holiness of angels or archangels but the archetypal holiness of God.

Charnock develops the following points regarding the goal to resemble God's holiness. To begin, the command to imitate divine holiness is not "an order to cease to be creatures, and commence to be gods," but rather an order to possess the same kind of holiness, rather than the essence of holiness. For mankind to possess the essence of God's holiness would be an impossibility. Charnock illustrates the difference of the two spheres of holiness: "a short line may be as straight as the other, though it parallel it not in the immense length of it."

In the same vein, Charnock recommends that believers not look to other believers for a template of holiness, but rather to God himself. "To endeavor to be like a good man is to make one image like another; to set our clocks by other clocks, without regarding the sun: but true holiness consists in a likeness to the most exact

57. IV:120.
58. IV:120, 123.
59. IV:121.
60. IV:122.
61. IV: 122.
62. IV:566.

sampler." Just as the Stoics looked to human examples of virtue, such as Socrates, Christians must look to the divine example of holiness, as manifest in Jesus.[63]

Regarding obedience to the law, Charnock argues that the motive for obeying God must be the will to imitate divine holiness, rather than a desire for health, security, or prosperity. First, we must perceive, and then conform to, the purity of God's nature. The purity of God's nature, though invisible to the human eye, is visible to us through his law; hence, it is law both "holy" (Romans 7:12) and "pure" (Psalm 19:8). By two metaphors, Charnock describes the law of God—a window and a transcript. Both metaphors imply that God's holiness is known through his law. Moreover, God's holiness may be imitated through conformity to his law. "Our lives," enjoins Charnock, are to be a "comment upon his law."[64]

In analyzing man's conformity to God's law, Charnock makes an insightful, profound distinction:

> If it [conformity to the law] be agreeable to God's will, and convenient for some design of our own, and we do anything only with a respect to this design, we make not God's holiness discovered in the law our rule, but our own conveniency: it is not a conformity to God, but a conformity of our actions to self.[65]

If for instance, one abstains from intemperance not because the law commands it but rather for health, one is not following God's holiness but a wish for one's own security, convenience, or whatever, then we are involved in making a god of ourselves. All that the believer does, therefore, must be an expression of divine holiness, as articulated in the law of God. True obedience is not a mere "resisting in negatives, but aspiring to positives."[66] All that believers do must accord with the positive goal of resembling God's purity.

63. II:199.
64. II:200.
65. II:200.
66. II:200.

CONCLUSION

The precision and depth of Charnock's understanding of God's law challenges the truncated, confused, and even self-contradictory understanding as interpreted by modern evangelicalism. While modern evangelicalism holds "not under law but under grace," it cries out for biblical principles from the Old Testament. Many claim that Old Testament law is "not for us" but regard all Scripture as profitable for doctrine, reproof, correction, and instruction in righteousness (2 Timothy 3:16). Charnock was unencumbered by such misled demands. Rather, to Charnock "we do not make void the law, rather we establish it" (Romans 3:31). Ceremonial law, according to Charnock, was brought to a higher state under Christ, though moral law and the general equity of the judicial law remain in force. To Charnock, the law of God was a viable force in every believer's life, in the life of the church at large, and in society.

Puritan luminaries examined God's law with a clarity of understanding we can only envy today, when we are much more the victims of muddled thinking. As a movement, Puritanism maintained a balance by exploring the relationship between law and grace. Through the law, Puritans awakened a need for divine grace in the hearts of believers. They used the law to convince people of the dangers of sin and their need of salvation. They highlighted the righteousness of Christ. They explained the duties required of Christians who seek sanctification. They explained what God requires of a civil magistrate. Such was their resolution and understanding; it is inviting to see it as an antidote for the loose beliefs of today. It may deflect the tide of antinomianism and worldliness that affects the visible church.

FINAL CONCLUSION

The passing of the Puritan era may prompt modern adherents to Puritan theology to lament – mourn the dissipations of what Charles Haddon Spurgeon called a religious "Augustan age." The classical period of the 5th century B.C. ancient Greece produced a remarkable genius-per-capita ratio; not dissimilarly, the Puritan period of the 17th century A.D. produced a remarkable theologian-per-capita ratio, with remaining works that have stood the scrutiny of time.

Harold J. Berman of Harvard corrects a misgiving as modern interpreters of Scripture may reminisce a bygone era:

> Merely to mourn the passing of an era would, of course, be foolish. Since there is no going back, the important question is "How shall we go forward?" By retracing the experience through which we arrived at our present predicament, can we find some guidelines, and some resources, that may help us to overcome the obstacles that block our way to the future?[1]

Berman sees that in the postmodern era, the degeneration of adherence to moral absolutes, the departure from moral norms, and the declension into a-moral chaos have exacerbated human pain. The post-modern moral compass points everywhere, with no true north.

---

1. Harold J. Berman, "Religious Foundations of Law in the West: An Historical Perspective," *Journal of Law and Religion*, Volume 1, Number 1, Summer 1983, p. 30.

FINAL CONCLUSION

As theologians in our own day debate and deliberate the continuity and discontinuity of the Testaments, the remaining, abiding light of the Puritans' grasp on the connection of the New and Older Testament remains of moment.

To be sure, abiding light bequeathed to the current theological academic community is too salient, and unique, to be ignored. If the Puritan divines struck a note of universal truth, quod omnium interest ab omnibus approbari debet. Universal truth should be considered by all. A sounded note of universal truth should be heard, and considered by all.

BIBLIOGRAPHY

Berman, Harold J. "Religious Foundations of Law in the West: An Historical Perspective." *Journal of Law and Religion*, Volume 1, Number 1, Summer 1983.

Flynn, John Stephen. *The Influence of Puritanism on the Political and Religious Thought of the English*. New York: E.P. Dutton, 1920.

Haller, William. *Liberty and Reformation in the Puritan Revolution*. New York: Columbia University Press, 1955.

Pearson, A.F. Scott. *Church and State—Political Aspects of Sixteenth Century Puritanism*. Cambridge: At the University Press, 1927.

Seaver, Paul S. *Journal of Church and State*, Volume 26, Number 1, Winter 1984.

Tatham, G.B. *The Puritans in Power—A Study in the History of the English Church from 1640 to 1660*. Cambridge: At the University Press, 1913.

Margo Todd, *Christian Humanism and the Puritan Social Order* (Cambridge: Cambridge University Press, 1987.

Zaret, David. *The Heavenly Contract—Ideology and Organization in Pre-Revolutionary Puritanism*. Chicago: The University of Chicago Press, 1985.

Wilson, John F. *Pulpit in Parliament*. Princeton, University Press, 1969.

www.ingramcontent.com/pod-product-compliance
Lightning Source LLC
Chambersburg PA
CBHW071436160426
43195CB00013B/1930